Jazz and Cricket

AN UNLIKELY COMBINATION

Matthew Wright

First published in 2021 by Cadillac Music & Publishing Ltd.

ISBN 978-1-5272-8259-9
British Library Cataloguing-in-Publication Data
A catalogue record for this book is available from the British Library

Cover design and typesetting © Stephen Morris 2021 www.stephen-morris.co.uk
Set in Minion Pro 11/13
Printed via Akcent Media

Contents

Preface

It was when I was working with Ray Smith at Collets Jazz Shop, years ago, that I first became aware of a number of people involved in jazz that had a deep interest in cricket. Ray played for the Ravers, a cricket club briefly mentioned in George Melly's book *Owning Up*, and I got to know several of the musicians/players. I also got to know Jim Godbolt well, helping him with several of his writing projects, and following the death of these two, I decided to enlarge on what Jim had written about his experiences in both the jazz and cricket worlds. Both Ray and Jim gave me valuable information and many photographs, some of which appear in this book. This modest volume is therefore dedicated to these two old friends, and to the late Neil Kellas, with whom I spent many hours discussing cricket and jazz, and with whom I occasionally played cricket for the Brown Bear cricket team in Deptford – enthusiastically rather than proficiently.

In this writing I have included a good deal of the background history of cricket in the areas of the world (West Indies, USA, South Africa) outside of Britain, where jazz was a major element in music, as I feel it important to get an idea of the social context in which both developed

I would like to thank the many people who have spoken to me when researching, but in particular Val Wilmer, not only for directing me towards areas I was not familiar with, but for her continued support and encouragement. Thanks also to Richard Williams, Howard Rye, Ron Gould, Orlando Le Fleming, Steve Beresford, Mike Gavin of Cadillac Music and to Mark Gilbert of *Jazz Journal* and Spike Wells for publishing short versions online. An earlier, brief one also appeared in *Wisden's* quarterly magazine, *The Nightwatchman* (Spring 2019).

Appreciation must also go to Vereena, Ellie, Emily and Joe, for their patience and toleration.

Matthew Wright, 2020

Introduction

Whenever the series of cricket matches known as The Ashes are played between England and Australia it reminds me of one day in 2013, when a small group of us left the Magdala pub in Hampstead to scatter the remains of writer, former agent and long-time editor of house magazine *Jazz at Ronnie Scott's*, Jim Godbolt. On our way to the Heath I noticed clarinettist Wally Fawkes had an earpiece plugged into a radio, and asked him what he was listening to. "Cricket," he appropriately replied, "The Ashes."

The links between cricket and music have been written about at some length, particularly by David Rayvern Allen, whose book *A Song For Cricket* (1981) is a comprehensive account covering the earliest references, through Victorian and Edwardian eras to the present. Cricket was widely represented in the world of music, one of the earliest had cricketers appeared on the title page of Matthias von Holst's *Village Rondo*, written in 1812 by Matthias Holst, great-grandfather of Gustav. Others include Peter Warlock's *Cricketers of Hambledon*, Alfred Scott-Gatty's *Cricket* (dedicated to the I Zingari club), and the Victorian ballroom dances, Charles T. West's *Ranjitsinhji Waltz*, Alfred Taylor's *The Merry Cricketers' Polka* and, dedicated to W.G. Grace, Henry Sutch's *Cricket Bat Polka*, right up to Roy Harper's 1975 metaphor for death, *When An Old Cricketer Leaves The Crease*, described by Allen as "in essence *the* cricket song."

Calypso, understandably, is also well covered in the book, as it is elsewhere, but little has appeared to document the affinity between cricket and jazz. Superficially they may seem light years apart – stereotypical ideas prevailing. Cricket may conjure up a picture of relatively healthy players engaged in a sedate, even dull game on a village green, whereas jazz has connotations of dimly-lit subterranean dives, full of hooded-eyed, spaced out modernists or knitted-jumper clad Trad jazz jivers. Of course, there may be a hint of truth in these, but both cricket and jazz have common elements – technical expertise and skill in playing, interaction with fellow players and response to their contributions, plus the opportunity for individual expression and improvisation within a structured context. In issue number 3 (1982) of the music magazine *Collusion*, pianist & saxophonist Jez Parfett extolled the virtues of the cricketer Kumar 'Prince' Ranjitsinhji, making this connection. A favourite of the crowds, he played for Sussex from 1895 and was a huge compiler of runs with a style unlike the traditional English approach, notably in his playing the ball very late and scoring heavily on the leg side, a feature which included his trademark leg glance. Parfett also recalled a day at the Oval in 1975, when he saw West Indian Alvin Kallicharran score 35 off ten deliveries from Australian Dennis Lillee in a one day international. "His astonishing improvisation ranged in dynamic contrast and tension from *sotto voce* to *con fuoco*, exhibiting *legato* and *staccato* articulation of the wrists in conjunction with savage percussion and multiphonic variation of stroke."

Writer Neville Cardus often saw parallels between the way cricketers performed and the arts, including music. He described the batting of George Gunn (1879-1958) as classic elements mixed with modernity and unorthodox improvisations, like "Louis Armstrong playing in the Philharmonic Orchestra while a symphony by Mozart was being performed." Supporting this is David Frith's comment about Gunn in *The Golden Age of Cricket 1890-1914* (1978): "A man of caprice, he sometimes blocked innocent balls because it pleased him, and sometimes went down the wicket to even the fastest bowling and did with it as he liked." Writing for the *Manchester Guardian* in the 1920s, Cardus remarked about Cecil Parkin (1886-1943) "In the age of jazz and Irving Berlin, Parkin became the first jazz cricketer – his slow ball was syncopation in flight." An inventive and often devastating off-spinner, who used flight, guile and turn to dismiss batsmen, no doubt helped by his prowess as an amateur conjuror and magician, he topped the Test averages against Warwick Armstrong's powerful Australian side in 1921. He delighted crowds with his eccentricities but was unpopular with the cricketing authorities, however, as his views, which as a part-time journalist he aired in print, were considered outspoken, especially in his criticism of class distinction and anti-northern bias in cricket. At one point his Lancashire and England captain Archie McLaren called for the suppression of this 'cricketing Bolshevist'! There was also the difficulty of setting fields to suit his unpredictable bowling, which irritated captains and subverted the code of the game.

More recently, Antiguan activist and journalist Tim Hector wrote that West Indian batsmen Gary Sobers and Rohan Kanhai "embodied what can really be termed the satyric passion for the expression of the natural man, bursting through the restraints of disciplined necessity. Both showed the creativity of the great jazz musicians in their marvellous improvisations." Hector regarded improvisation in jazz as *the* innovation in twentieth-century music. Jim Godbolt also acknowledged a direct connection between the sport and the music: "Both cricket and jazz, irrespective of style, require a strong sense of rhythm, timing, concentration, improvisation, solo and team work." (*All This and Slowly Deteriorating Fast*, 2013)

Music and sports writer Richard Williams made the simple point connecting the two: "I like it when nobody, neither the participants nor the audience, knows what's going to happen or how it's going to turn out, which is the link between cricket and jazz." An opinion mirrored by classical composer Harrison Birtwistle, a regular visitor to Lord's, described by Stephen Fay in the *Magazine of Marylebone Cricket Club* (Autumn/Winter 2011) as a spectator who does not care much about who wins or loses, and who judges individual performances in the same way he would make an artistic judgement of a musician's performance. Unpredictability is an essential element in his scores, the composer explained, his pieces are not just built around themes that develop and repeat (as in traditional classical music), just as cricket can be improvised within the formal framework of overs and innings. "To Birtwistle," wrote Fay, "the charm of both cricket and his music is that the spectator can never be sure what is about to happen."

George Gunn

On the sleeve notes to *Eric Dolphy in Europe* (1964), the saxophonist and flautist is quoted as saying "There's always been something else to strive for. The more possibilities of new things I hear, it's like I'll never stop finding sounds I hadn't thought existed until just now." This could be likened to the cricketer who is constantly exploring new ways of playing, either responding to an opposing batsman or bowler, or attempting to change the direction of the game according to how the player wants it to go. There is a series of events, each single one has possibilities and it is within this context that individuals can express themselves. Within the perform-ance of the band or the team, personnel can change, maintaining the structure of the whole but allowing for individual and different contributions which might poten-

Cecil Parkin

tially alter the rendition and execution. The total spectacle can be seen as consisting of a series of individual, isolated episodes, each in itself self-contained. According to how these are performed defines the fluctuating rise and fall within the game (or piece of music). As David Toop, in his book *Into the Maelstrom: Music, Improvisation and the Dream of Freedom* (2016) observed, "improvisation determines the outcomes of events," referring to music, but of course this applies to cricket. There might be a logical progression, according to the 'rules' of music, which reinforces what is accepted. Improvisation doesn't necessarily follow this. It can open up a wider field of potentiality. It attempts not be impeded by the baggage of musical scores and techniques, although it may use the latter to enhance or widen the performance. Years of repetitive practice and consequent mastery of an instrument can enable the player to react quickly, almost subconsciously, in a given situation, when faced with circumstances which necessitate immediate response; cricketers can also find themselves in that position.

"The personal achievement may be of the utmost competence or brilliance," wrote C.L.R. James in *Beyond a Boundary* (1963), "Its ultimate value is whether it assists the side to victory or staves off defeat." As during a band's performance of a piece of music, an inspired solo lends itself to the success of the whole rendition, the soloist using intuitive and learned techniques to produce something that will achieve this. "Cricket is first and foremost a dramatic spectacle. It belongs with the theatre, ballet, opera and the dance." Renowned cricketer C.B. Fry is credited with the epigram "Batting is a dance with a stick in your hand". When reproached for being a batsman with only one stroke, replied "Yes, but I could make the ball go to ten different parts of the field."

The dramatic element may be characterised in the way two individuals are pitted against each other – the batsman and the bowler – but also in the way each represents their side. The value of personal achievement is whether it assists the side to victory or helps avoid defeat. He may or may not succeed, but for that moment "the batsman facing the ball does not merely represent his side... he is his side." (James) Just like Bubber Miley or Johnny Hodges during a solo in front of the full Duke Ellington Orchestra.

1

Early West Indies Cricket

Given the historical transatlantic connection between the US, Caribbean and Britain it should come as no great surprise that there would be cultural links. Certainly there are arguments, such as those put forward by Keith Sandiford (with Brian Stoddart: *The Imperial Game: Cricket, Culture and Society,* 1998) and others, that cultural imperialism was largely responsible for cricket being played between the West Indies and England, the colonials introducing sporting and recreational models. This extended to all parts of the Empire, and in *Cricket and Race* (2001) Jack Williams examines this aspect closely, making the point that in late colonial times, of the Victorian and Edwardian eras, cricket played a role in how the English were perceived, and perhaps more importantly, how they wanted to be perceived, and as an expression of their moral values and what they saw as their essential qualities. This of course was from the position of authority, colonial domination and rule, plus the assumptions of racial superiority. It was borne out by the comments of Lord Selborne, Under-Secretary of State for the Colonies, who said at a dinner given to the West Indian touring team at the West Indian Club in 1900, of the importance played by sport and cricket in particular, which "had a real influence in harmonising and consolidating the different parts of the Empire." (*The Times*, 14 August 1900) It wasn't only the English who inclined to this view. Surrey and MCC member J.M. Framjee Patel, a leading figure in Parsee cricket in India, was quoted as saying "Let cricket be one of the many links to unite the citizens of the greatest Empire the world has ever seen. Let the providential alliance of India and Britain be cemented with the lasting and enduring ties of one peace-loving King-Emperor, one beautiful language, one victorious flag but not least, one grand Imperial game." (*Cricket*, June 1906) Contentious, and just what the British rulers would like to hear, but with one element that strikes a chord – that of the ability of cricket to unite people.

Although cricket was played in Denmark, Holland, Germany and the USA, it was recognised as being associated with those countries in the British Empire and was developed through those British whites stationed in the far outposts of the Empire and through the settlers. Although primarily white, it also included non-white participation, although the extent of this tended to be localised.

Cricket was introduced into the West Indies through the British military, who established clubs and garrison teams. The first references seem to be from a diary entry by a Jamaican slave owner called Thistlewood that cricket was played in 1778, a mention in the *Barbados Mercury and Bridgetown Gazette* in 1806, and the discovery, in 1979, of a belt buckle featuring what appears to be an Afro-European slave playing cricket in Barbados dating from *c*1780. As cricket was played in cane fields, slaves were given the task of retrieving the ball and throwing it back, so from there it developed into them being involved in the game and sometimes encouraged. This encounter of slaves with cricket was supported by former Jamaican Prime Minister Michael Manley: "the young sons of the slaves were required to bowl at the young sons of the slave owners or to the army officers... of course the sons of the slaves practised batting in their spare time." (*History of West Indian Cricket*, 1995)

The planters used the game in an attempt to divert attention away from social unrest, hoping its moral codes, values and behavioural standards would help in this respect. By 1840 many were staging games on their plantations and teams and clubs started to appear, although different ones for aristocratic whites, merchant-class whites, coloureds (mulattos), and blacks. Racial integration for the most part during this time was not allowed. Inter-island competitions took place; the first was between Demerara and Barbados in 1865. Gradually, inter-racial games became more common although segregation still occurred to a large extent. An early musical connection was mentioned in *Cricket* (28 March 1895) in its report of a match played by R.S. Lucas' touring team in the West Indies, when a local musician accompanied each batsman to the wicket, "with musical honours of the weirdest description, produced by a sort of clarinet."

International cricket, predominantly white at first, was organised around the 1880s when the first West Indies team was formed and which toured Canada and the US, then played Lord Hawke's visiting England team in the 1890s. The first official Test match between the two was not until 1926, although there were tours of England in 1900, when the white Trinidadian, Aucher Warner, the brother of future England captain Pelham Warner, led a touring side, and then in 1906, under Harold Austin. These played a number of county teams. The Marylebone Cricket Club, which had taken over responsibility for arranging all official overseas England tours, visited the West Indies in 1910-11 and 1912-13 but after that there was no international cricket of any note until the West Indian team went to England in 1923.

It was then that the first apparent link between jazz and West Indian cricket began, with a gathering of a group in London known as the 'Coterie of Friends'. This was set up in 1919 by American clarinettist and composer Edmund Jenkins (1894-1926), the son of Rev. Daniel Joseph Jenkins who founded Jenkins Orphanage in Charleston, South Carolina. The younger Jenkins played in and directed the Orphanage's bands, whose alumni were to include trumpeters Freddie Jenkins, William 'Cat' Anderson and Jabbo Smith, songwriter and pianist Tom Delaney and guitarist Freddie Green (who was to become well-known as a member of Count Basie's rhythm section). After training at college in Atlanta, Georgia with Kemper Harreld (also the tutor of Fletcher Henderson), Jenkins went to England with the orphanage band in 1914, to play at the Anglo-American Exposition, and remained there studying at the Royal Academy of Music from 1914 to 1921. During this time he played with Will Marion Cook's Southern Syncopated Orchestra, which also included Sidney Bechet.

He became familiar with the game of cricket, mainly through Caribbean friends and his connection with Thomas H. Jackson and Dr. Felix 'Harry' Leekam. Jackson was the editor of the Nigerian newspaper *Lagos Weekly Record*, and who, like Jenkins, had been involved with the African Progress Union, as well as being a member

Original programme for Coterie of Friends, *courtesy Howard Rye*

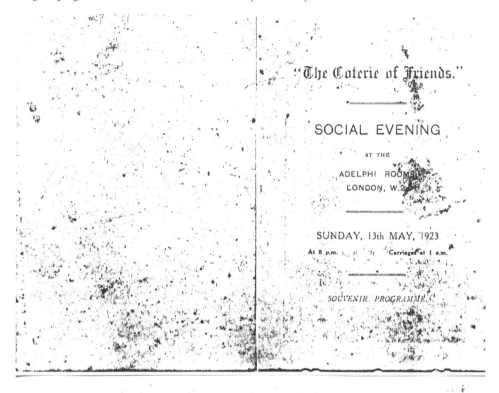

"The Coterie of Friends."

SOCIAL EVENING

AT THE

ADELPHI ROOMS
LONDON, W.2

SUNDAY, 13th MAY, 1923

At 8 p.m. :: :: Carriages at 1 a.m.

SOUVENIR PROGRAMME

"The Coterie of Friends."

The above is the name of a Club started by a small group of Students with the object of creating a social vehicle whereby the much isolated population of serious, minded people of colour may come into contact at frequent intervals. Though dormant for the past twelve months or more (owing to the departure from London of some of its principal members) the Club can claim the credit of having given, during the period of its activity, social functions foremost in the Negro world of London.

Following are the names of the original members and founders :

EDMUND T. JENKINS, A.R.A.M., President.
HAROLD. R. PIPER, F.C.L., Secretary.
FELIX H. LEEKAM, L.C.P., Vice-President.
RANDALL H. LOCKHART, Treasurer.
A. LUKE.
J. McDOUGALL.

GUESTS OF HONOUR.

Miss FLORENCE MILLS

Mr. WILL VODERY

Mr. SHELTON BROOKES

Mr. JAMES P. JOHNSON
and his Orchestra who have kindly taken charge of the Musical Programme.

Members of the West Indian Cricket Team.

Honorary M.C. - Mr. LEYLAND HARPER.

Organisers :

Mr. EDMUND T. JENKINS

Dr. FELIX H. LEEKAM.

of Essex CCC. Leekam was a keen cricketer, regularly watched Middlesex and would have known of the visit to England in 1922 of Harold Austin, to arrange a visit of the West Indies team the following year. The West Indian's 1923 cricket tour did not include a game against an England team, but played against many of the county teams and played at Cambridge on 19 May, coincidentally the same day that Jenkins hired an "omnibus and extra man" from Thomas Wolfe's garage in Woburn Square, which according to Jeffrey Green (*Edmund Thornton Jenkins – The Life & Times of an American Black Composer,* 1982) "may well have been for yet another of his American and Caribbean gatherings." For a day trip to Cambridge perhaps? There was also an end-of-season game against HDG Leveson-Gower's XI against a virtual England Test side at the Scarborough cricket festival, which Leveson-Gower's XI won by only four wickets. Playing for Gower's team was the mercurial Cecil Parkin, who took 5 for 36 in the West Indies' second innings, no doubt bearing out Cardus' comments as being "the first jazz cricketer." Of the 20 first-class matches played on the tour, 6 matches were won, 7 were lost and 7 were drawn. In all matches 13 were won, 7 were lost and 8 were drawn.

In the spring and summer of 1923, two African-American companies appeared in London in what was known collectively as *Plantation Revues.* The first to arrive was the cast of *Plantation Days*, at Plymouth on March 12, from New York City aboard the Red Star Liner, *Finland*. It had played in Chicago, Indianapolis and other American cities and included the vaudeville blues singer Josephine Carter, who had recorded for Okeh in 1921, and the eminent and influential figure in early jazz, pianist James P. Johnson and his Orchestra, in which were clarinettist and violinist Darnell Howard and future Duke Ellington bassist/trombonist Wellman Braud (named as 'Brand' on the official list). During the London stay, the orchestra was to accompany Fred and Adele Astaire at Ciro's Club and Wellman Braud apparently sat in at Moody's Club in Tottenham Court Road, a regular venue for black bands at the time.

On 10 May, the *Plantation Revue* from Sam Salvin's Plantation Restaurant in New York City arrived at King George V Docks in London, aboard the Cunard liner, *Albania*. In this were the cabaret singer, dancer and entertainer Florence Mills, composer and singer Shelton Brooks, blues singer Edith Wilson and Will Vodery's Plantation Orchestra. When it opened as *From Dover Street to Dixie*, reviews were mixed, although Spike Hughes was later to write (as 'Mike' for the *Melody Maker*, 23 April 1938) "my friends tell me that their (Will Vodery's Orchestra) opening of the coloured half was one of the musical events of the century." For the details of these tours, a comprehensive account was written by Howard Rye in *Storyville* magazine 133 entitled *Visiting Firemen 13: The Plantation Revues* (March 1988).

On Sunday 13 May, the week before the likely excursion to Cambridge, Edmund Jenkins and his friend Harry Leekam organised a Social Evening at the Adelphi Hotel, London, for the Coterie of Friends. The purpose of the Coterie of Friends was to create "a social vehicle whereby the much isolated population of serious minded people of colour may come into contact at frequent intervals." (Coterie of Friends programme notes.) The guests of honour included Florence Mills, Will Vodery Shelton Brooks and James P. Johnson, whose Orchestra had "kindly taken charge of the Musical Programme." Also as guests of honour were members of the West Indian Cricket Team, who had arrived in late April and included the young 22-year-old Learie Constantine. In the audience were singer and vaudeville star, Nora Bayes, and Paul Whiteman, often referred to, somewhat controversially, as the 'King of Jazz'.

The talented Jenkins was one of the first composers to merge the folk songs and music of the black South with European orchestral traditions; his *Folk Rhapsody (On American Folk Tunes)* was premiered in London in 1919 at the Coleridge-Taylor Orchestral Concert, hosted by the Coterie of Friends. It referenced the African-American spirituals *Swing Low Sweet Chariot* and *Nobody Knows the Trouble I've Seen*. Another paid tribute to his native city, *American Folk Rhapsody: Charlestonia*. An accomplished musician, he regularly played clarinet and saxophone in the Queen's Dance Orchestra, with Jack Hylton on piano, and often visited Paris to perform in clubs and concerts. As Will Marion Cook wrote in a letter to the Rev. Jenkins:

> Want to congratulate you on your son... with whom I had a most wonderful association while in Paris. He is possibly the best musician in the coloured race, the very best instrumentalist in any race, and one of the most perfect gentlemen I have ever had the pleasure of knowing.

Jenkins died in Paris in 1926, from complications following an operation for appendicitis. He was 33.

2

Undergraduates and School Connections

When Cambridge undergraduate Maurice Allom exchanged his saxophone for a cricket ball, he was to make sporting history. Born in Northwood, Middlesex on 23 March 1906, Allom attended Wellington College, Berkshire before going to Cambridge University, for whom he played cricket between 1926 and 1928. He went on to play for Surrey from 1927 to 1937 and for England in 5 test matches.

During his time at Cambridge, he joined the band of pianist Fred Elizalde, as a saxophonist. Elizalde was an interesting figure. Born Federico Elizalde in Navarro, Spain, in 1907, to a family of wealthy plantation owners in the Philippines, he studied piano at the Madrid Royal Conservatory before being sent to Stanford (USA) with his brother Lizz (Manuel) to study law. Lizz moved to Cambridge, England, to continue his studies and joined the Quinquaginta Band, playing alto sax. Fred soon followed and took over leadership of the band, changing its name to the Quinquaginta Ramblers, and in 1927 it made four sides for Brunswick, as Fred Elizalde and His 'Varsity Band.

Fred Elizalde (p,arr), John d'Arcy Hildyard (t), Dick Battle (t,fh), Manuel Elizalde, Jack Donaldson (cl,ss,as), 'Dan' Wyllie (as,bsx), Maurice Allom (cl,as,ts,bar), George Cosmo Monkhouse (bj,g), 'Bud' Williams (bb), Eric Sandars (d).

Rec. Shepherd's Bush, London, March 30, 1927
1. High-High-High Up In The Hills (Lewis-Young-Abrahams) Br 1000
2. Muddy Water (Trent-de Rose-Richman) Br 1000
3. Ain't She Sweet (Yellen-Ager)   Br 1001
4. Hurricane (Mertz & Nichols) Br 1001

Then, as Fred Elizalde and His Cambridge Undergraduates, two sides were made for HMV:

Same personnel. Hayes, Middlesex, June 22, 1927
5. Bb-11050-1 Stomp Your Feet (Elizalde)   HMV B-5315
6. Bb-11051-2 Clarinet Marmalade (Shields & Ragas)   HMV B-5315

Edgar Jackson reviewed "Clarinet Marmalade/Stomp Your Feet" for the Melody Maker (October 1927) describing the "outstanding instrumentalists on the record" and mentioning Maurice Allom, "the famous cricket Blue" playing tenor saxophone. On listening to it, not all would agree.

"Even allowing for the poor standard of recording in those days the whole effect was messy," wrote contemporary Harry Francis some years later (ref. *National Jazz Archives*), "it being clear that the amateur musicians were attempting to play arrangements that required a standard of ability far in excess of their own."

However, Allom was destined for greater things as was Elizalde, who continued with a more competent and influential band, playing at the Savoy and featuring some of the best players in early British jazz, including Jack Jackson, Harry Hayes and Buddy Featherstonhaugh, as well as Americans Chelsea Quealey, Fud Livingston, Adrian Rollini and Arthur Rollini. In the 1930s, Elizalde worked in Biarritz, Paris and Madrid and was associated with composers Maurice Ravel, Darius Milhaud and Manuel de Falla, and collaborated with Spanish poet Federico Garcia Lorca. During the Spanish Civil War he became a captain in Franco's army and was wounded. After this he moved to Manila then France, where he lived in confinement near Bayonne during the German occupation. He was later to lead the London Symphony Orchestra at the Royal Festival Hall during the Festival of Britain.

Meanwhile, Allom's cricketing career was to flourish as a medium-fast bowler who at 6'6" height, was able to get the ball to rise sharply off the pitch. His first successful season was in 1927 when he recorded his best performance in taking 9 wickets for 55 runs for Cambridge University versus The Army.

As *Wisden* for that year recounts, he "proved so deadly that in eight overs and a ball he took seven wickets at a cost of 9 runs. Allom followed up this startling performance by disposing of five batsmen in the second innings, his full record for the match being fourteen wickets for just over 7 runs apiece. He had two men leg before, and hit the stumps eleven times."

In the same season he played against a very strong Yorkshire team, taking 7 – 98 in their first innings (out of a total of 382) then a further two wickets out of the three to fall in their second innings. These included the wickets of Percy Holmes, who had scored 315 not out against Middlesex in 1925; Herbert Sutcliffe (twice), the first cricketer to score 16 centuries in test match cricket; Edgar Oldroyd (twice), who writer John Arlott credited as "the best sticky-wicket batsman in the world"; and all-rounder Wilfred Rhodes, who completed the double of 1000 runs and 100 wickets in an English cricket season 16 times. These were class players and an indication of Allom's skill as a bowler.

Allom's greatest feat was to come when he was called up by England in 1930, for the tour of New Zealand. As his obituary in *Wisden* was later to say, "With one sensational over at Lancaster Park, Christchurch in January 1930, Maurice Allom joined the immortals." The first ball of his eighth over saw batsman Roger Blunt narrowly escape an LBW decision, and a leg bye was taken. The second ball he bowled Stuart Dempster. New Zealand captain Tom Lowry played and missed the third ball, but was out on the fourth ball, leg before wicket. Allom's fifth ball had Ken James caught by wicketkeeper Tich Cornford and he clean bowled Ted Badcock with his sixth. Allom finished with figures of 19 overs, 4 maidens, 5 wickets for 38 runs, becoming the first bowler to take a hat-trick (3 wickets in 3 successive balls) on Test debut and also the first to take 4 Test wickets in 5 deliveries.

Surrey 1932, Maurice Allom is front row second left, sitting between Jack Hobbs and Douglas Jardine

Allom was to play in only five Tests, but continued with Surrey until his retirement in 1937. He was later to become President of the MCC in 1969-70, during which period the issue of the South African tour to England arose. Following the Basil D'Oliviera affair, Allom argued in *The Times* that it wasn't the South African Cricket authorities that opposed the inclusion of D'Oliviera in England's touring team in 1968, but the government, that South African cricketers had always "been keen to play with and against cricketers of any race wherever and whenever they can," reflecting the naive argument that sports only become political when politicians intervene. The opposition to the proposed 1970 South African tour was spearheaded by the Anti-Apartheid Movement, members of the Labour government and eminent figures such as ex-England cricketer the Rev. David Sheppard, Lord Learie Constantine and Father Trevor Huddleston. The English Cricket Council, the governing body of cricket, wisely changed their mind and "By cancelling the tour, the Cricket Council helped to ensure that Test cricket would continue as a multi-racial sport and not split into separate white and non-white groups." (*Cricket and Race*, Jack Williams, 2001)

Allom died in 1995, *The Times* obituary adding that during that turbulent time:

Allom never lost his benign, cheerful and kindly attitude to his fellow men, even those who were causing him a great deal of trouble.

Maurice Allom's cricket career statistics:

Tests: 5 matches
Batting average 14.00
Bowling : 14 wickets for 265 runs   Average 18.92
First Class: 179 matches
Batting average 12.84
Bowling : 605 wickets for 14291 runs   Average 23.62

In contrast to Allom, Cambridge undergraduate (albeit briefly} Patrick 'Spike' Hughes' talents lay more in music. Born in 1908, his father, Herbert Hughes, was an Irish/Ulster musician/songwriter who became music editor of the *Daily Telegraph* and founder of the Irish Folksong Society. Patrick's mother was artistic but can be best described as a traveller, sometime teacher, sometime explorer. As a young child Patrick spent his childhood travelling with his mother and gaining a wide musical experience. In the first volume of his autobiography, *Opening Bars* (1946), he recalls, whilst living in Vienna in 1924, seeing the black jazz performer Bo-Bo and his Band and the following year he saw American jazz trumpeter Arthur Briggs and his band playing at the Weinburg Bar.

Back in England Hughes settled down in Cambridge as an undergraduate, although it didn't last very long. His interest in cricket had begun when he was young, playing at school, and he saw Warwick Armstrong's Australians playing Sussex at Hove in 1921, when Dick Young scored 124 against the visitors and Hughes' hero Maurice Tate picked up 4 wickets for 21. Determined that this was what he wanted to do, Hughes' cricket "career", such that it was, began in 1926, when he spent "three afternoons a week in the nets at the Perse ground, bowling for hours on end and in the late afternoon being allowed to have a knock" (*Opening Bars*). The coach was John O'Connor, who had played for Derbyshire at the turn of the century. Hughes later recalled, "O'Connor was never a coach to try and alter a player's natural game, and I feel he would have been delighted to have seen me play the innings which, years later, I played in Sussex. It was an innings of such perfection that I despair of ever being able to repeat it. It lasted precisely three balls, and I played the same stroke to each. The first ball I missed, the second I hit clean over an oak tree for six, and the third bowled me all ends up. I have occasionally totalled more runs in an innings (I once made 39 against the band from the Hammersmith Palais de Danse), but I have never batted more satisfyingly nor more characteristically."

Hughes got the opportunity to bowl in the Cambridgeshire County nets and was chosen to play for the county against Huntingdonshire on 23 June 1926. Unfortunately he was out first ball and didn't get a chance to bowl. There was no record of it in *Wisden*, as it wasn't a championship game. He was to abandon his early cricketing ambitions for what he termed 'Coarse Cricket.' This, he wrote, was "notable more for the enthusiasm than the skill of its players and is best played against breweries." One of his proudest cricketing memories was in a charity game, "capturing the wickets of both Flanagan and Allen in one innings. This is undoubtedly a record."

He was also later to play for the *Daily Herald* against a team headed by Maurice Tate, in 1938. He bowled unchanged and helped dismiss Tate's XI for 17, taking 6 wickets for 9 runs. However, the greatest satisfaction for him came from square-cutting his boyhood idol for four. "I know Maurice was playing in carpet slippers, for he had a septic foot, but even so a dream came no less true for all that." Another cricketing story Hughes recalled was from 1940 and "a startling action photograph of me fielding in the gully which appeared in *The Sporting and Dramatic*." This was during the first game ever played by the British Empire XI against Rosslyn Park for the prize of a barrel of beer. Having won, Hughes' team found that the barrel had been left out in the sun all day and was quite undrinkable.

In 1927 he saw the revue Blackbirds which featured Florence Mills and more importantly for him, Edith Wilson, who belted out "If you can't hold the man you love, don't cry when he's gone..." At this time he was also hearing many of the new jazz records coming out of the USA, thanks to his visits to Levy's Gramophone Shop in Whitechapel, and he became particularly impressed by Fletcher Henderson, Duke Ellington, Bix Beiderbecke, Eddie Lang and Adrian Rollini. Up until then he had been immersed in classical music and composition – by 1928 he wanted to master an instrument himself, so when a friend left a string bass in his apartment, he taught himself to play it. His first work was with Al Starita's Dance Band, then after a spell in France, found himself playing at the Cafe De Paris. His friendship with the composer William Walton resulted in him being introduced to Philip Lewis, recording manager for Decca, and soon Hughes was appointed as leader of their house band, which became known as Spike Hughes and his Decca-Dents.

They made many recordings from 1930 onwards, including some with American saxophonist Jimmy Dorsey (as Spike Hughes and his Three Blind Mice). His recordings, simply as Spike Hughes and his Orchestra, included trombonist Jock Fleming, whose son Bruce was to become an eminent jazz photographer in the 1960s, and clarinettist and saxophonist Harry Hines, who later umpired cricket matches and led his own novelty band, Dr.Crock and his Crackpots. Hughes optimistically asked Hines to play "like Jimmy Dorsey." After working in a revue for Charles Cochran in 1931, he formed close friendships with West Indian trumpet player and bassist Leslie Thompson and singer Joey Shields, who both subsequently played in his bands and recorded at Decca's Chenil Galleries. "Those records don't sound so adventurous now," recalled Thompson in *Swing From a Small Island : The Story of Leslie Thompson* (1985), "but in 1930 and 1931 they had a high reputation."

Around this time he also was offered work writing for the *Melody Maker*, then edited by Dan Ingham, a drummer who had worked with Percival Mackey and others at Decca, and he assumed the identity of 'Mike', writing and reviewing records. During his work with Jack Hylton's band, which included tours to Paris, Amsterdam and Brussels, Hughes struck up a close friendship with pianist Billy Munn, with whom he wrote *Six Bells Stampede*, a tribute to the musicians who regularly headed for the Six Bells pub, around the corner from the Chenil Galleries where Decca had its studios in Chelsea.

A big break came in 1932, when he was asked to orchestrate for Noel Coward's revue *Words and Music,* which opened at the Adelphi in September of that year. It included the famous songs *Mad Dogs and Englishmen* and *Mad About The Boy.* Hughes was paid £500, a very large amount in those days, and was wondering about a holiday, when saxophonist Buddy Featherstonhaugh suggested he went to America.

In January 1933, Hughes set off for New York and stayed with critic and producer John Hammond at his apartment in Greenwich Village. He had been introduced to Hammond in London by Edgar Jackson of the *Melody Maker.* On the first day in New York they went uptown to Harlem to meet Benny Carter rehearsing his band and Hughes struck up a friendship with him. Carter's band was to record *Six Bells Stampede* that year. During his stay in New York, Hughes saw Bessie Smith perform several times at Lafayettes Theatre, describing her singing as "not for the squeamish" but finding her rendition of *Empty Bed Blues* a moving experience. The Cotton Club was a huge disappointment for him though, notably as the audience was all white. However, he was enthusiastic about the Savoy Ballroom and Small's Paradise, where he heard trumpeter Henry Red Allen and tenor saxophonist Chu Berry. Hammond took him to see Art Tatum and within a few days they had persuaded Brunswick to record Tatum's piano solos. Hughes visited the Onyx Club, where he met Benny Goodman, Tommy Dorsey and renewed his friendship with Tommy's brother, Jimmy, and Monette's Supper Club, where Hammond introduced him to Billie Holiday.

Whilst in New York, Hughes called Decca and suggested he made some recordings with an all-black band for Brunswick, with whom Decca had an arrangement. Fourteen sides were recorded at 1776 Broadway and issued as Spike Hughes and his Negro Orchestra (later renamed Spike Hughes and his All-American Orchestra). Those involved included trombonist Dickie Wells, saxophonists Benny Carter, Chu Berry and Coleman Hawkins, pianist Luis Russell and trumpeter Henry Red Allen. Hawkins' solos were particularly excellent, Hughes describing them as "masterpieces of invention." Some of the scores were testing for players even of this calibre, Dickie Wells telling Stanley Dance in 1971, "No one in the outfit had the idea that he had so much hell in that valise until we started rehearsing. It was a good thing he had a gang like he had – these were cats who could see around a corner."

It was the fulfilment of an ambition for Hughes and he realised anything that came later would be an anti-climax. "I never played the double bass again... I left jazz behind me at the moment when I was enjoying it the most, the moment when all love affairs should end." When he left New York in May 1933, Duke Ellington's band was preparing to visit Britain. Hughes wrote an article about Duke which was published in the *Daily Herald* and this proved to be another turning point in his life as he stopped being a musician and became a writer, continuing as 'Mike' for the *Melody Maker,* and contributing to *The Daily Herald* and *The Times.* He started to turn to wider journalistic fields and also worked for the BBC, as a composer and as the author of a number of books, mainly on opera but including *The Art of Coarse Cricket* (1954). He eventually stopped being an influence in the development of jazz in Britain, but had certainly made a mark, not least for bringing to greater attention the considerable talents of such musicians as Coleman Hawkins, Red Allen, Dickie Wells and Benny Carter.

A potential connection that didn't quite develop was during the summer of 1936 when an Eton schoolmaster, George Lyttelton, took his wife and their fifteen year old son, Humphrey, to the Eton versus Harrow game at Lord's. Halfway through the game Mrs. Lyttelton and the son left the ground and got a taxi to a musical instrument shop in the Charing Cross Road, where the young man was bought a Deluxe Selmer trumpet. They returned to Lord's, the son by then totally disinterested in the cricket, no doubt dreaming of the future and what it might have in store for him. In later years, his interest in cricket was minimal, despite being surrounded by those – including Wally Fawkes, Bruce Turner, George Webb and others – who held different ideas about it.

3

London's Caribbean and African Community

In the 1930s, Jigs Club, run by Alec and Rose Ward and George 'Happy' Blake in Soho's Wardour Street, served as a sports and social club for London's Afro-Caribbean community as well as a music venue. It welcomed visiting musicians – the minutes of the committee meeting for Monday 17 July 1932 read: "as a special honour it was proposed to give Mr. Louis Armstrong and his band a complimentary dinner after his triumph at the London Palladium." The club was to be "renovated in the new year in readiness for the arrival of the West Indian Cricket Team." In 1933 the British West Indies Cricket Club players were met on their arrival at Tilbury on Easter Monday by members of the club, invited to dinner, "in honour of their visit" according to an entry in the day book, and made honorary members, as was Duke Ellington and his band, during the extent of their stay in the country. The Ellington Orchestra recorded four sides for Decca at the Chenil Galleries, Chelsea in the July of that year (*Hyde Park*; *Harlem Speaks; Ain't Misbehavin'; Chicago*).

The West Indian team included Jamaican batsman George Headley, one of *Wisden*'s Cricketers of the Year for 1934 and Trinidadian Clifford Roach, whose 180 against Surrey in 170 minutes was described by *Wisden* as the most dazzling innings on the tour, Roach scoring a century before lunch.

The writer C.L.R. James in *Beyond a Boundary* (1963) extolled the virtues of Headley, making a comparison with Learie Constantine, describing Constantine as a magician who was the product of tradition and training, whereas Headley was more of a natural cricketer. "Having taken a glance around, and sized up what the bowler is trying to do, the great batsman puts the ball away more by reflex than conscious action." This could be seen as not far removed from a jazz musician, formally trained at an academy or conservatoire in how to construct and play a solo, compared to one who has the capacity to improvise more instinctively and intuitively.

Despite individual exceptions, West Indian cricket was yet to reach the heights it was later to and playing failure by West Indian teams was often attributed to their temperament, even by writer Neville Cardus. In his book *Cricket* (1930) he drew a comparison between West Indian cricket and jazz:

> The West Indians in truth are jazz cricketers. That is to say, they give us a vivid sense of that improvisatory and far from formal energy which is the essence of jazz.

Like other commentators he tended to see the character as being erratic and a product of ethnicity. Often admiration was shown for their cricketing abilities, but too often it came accompanied by condescension, citing racial differences and character. There were those, however, who disagreed, notably C.L.R. James, who for example stated that

WEST INDIES CRICKET TEAM, 1933

LEFT TO RIGHT STANDING-
E. MARTINDALE.   F. R. MARTIN.   C. MERRY.   V. A. VALENTINE.   I. BARROW.   O DA COSTA.   E. ACHONG
SITTING-   H. C GRIFFITH.   E. L. G HOAD.   J. M. KIDNEY.   G. C. GRANT.   C. A. WILES.   C. A. ROACH
(MNGR).   (CAPT).
FRONT-   B. SEALY.   C. M. CHRISTIANI.   G. HEADLEY

Headley's ability was not based on ethnicity but on his skills. Constantine also was sceptical, questioning the idea of players being temperamental but rather that disunity was more the reason for poor results, especially the appointment of white captains on the basis of colour rather than merits of cricketing or leadership skills.

Bandleader Sam Manning, in the country at the time, and bassist Al Jennings, both from Trinidad, would no doubt have been interested in the progress of the 1933 touring team, as would trumpeter Leslie Thompson, who was a leading figure in London's Caribbean jazz community and a cricket enthusiast. Soon after his arrival from Jamaica in 1929, Thompson met and played with Al Jennings and pianist George Clapham, who had been with Will Marion Cook's Southern Syncopated Orchestra in 1920 and who was arrested with Sidney Bechet in 1922 for assault; Bechet was deported, Clapham avoided this as he was a British national. During his illustrious career Thompson was to play and record with Louis Armstrong in Paris in 1934 and tour Italy. "We had no programme in a formal sense," he was to recall in *Swing From a Small Island: The Story of Leslie Thompson* (1985)," for Louis felt what the audience was like, and played to them." It was testament to Thompson's musicianship that he was able to operate on this level.

In 1929 he met Dr. James Jackson Brown, "the first resident coloured person I met in England". Thompson had "stiff fingers" due to the cold weather and his landlady recommended him to Brown, who lived in Lauriston Road, near Victoria Park, East London. Originally from Jamaica, the doctor treated many of London's West Indian community and had even founded a cricket team, mainly made up of medical and law students and doctors. One day Al Jennings took Thompson out to Essex County Cricket playing fields by car, where J.J. Brown's West Indian cricket team were playing. It was the first time Thompson had seen English cricket, and wrote, "I suppose this was the summer of 1930. Some of those West Indian boys could play and I heard the Essex team talking about one fielder who was rushing about and catching one fellow here, and fielding brilliantly there, that they would have to watch him when Brown's team went in to bat. He was like greased lightning." Unfortunately Thompson doesn't say who this was. Through Brown he also met Louis Drysdale, a voice coach, whose main claim to fame was having given tuition to Florence Mills around 1923. Coincidentally, one of his pupils was the wife of a former associate of Edmund Jenkins, Dr. Harry Leekam, who played in Brown's cricket team.

Later, Trinidadians Carl Barriteau, George Roberts, Dave 'Baba' Williams and Dave Wilkins, were all recruited into the Thompson/Ken 'Snakehips' Johnson's band. According to writer Val Wilmer, Wilkins was particularly interested in cricket, both watching and playing. Born in Barbados in 1914, he decided to play the trumpet after hearing records by Bix Beiderbecke and by 1934 was playing with Bert McLean's Jazz Hounds. He came to London to join the Johnson band in 1937 and played and recorded extensively during the 1940s. During the 50s he was associated with Club Eleven and the British bop players, following which he played with the bands of Joe Mudele, Bruce Turner and Wally Fawkes, all very keen followers and players of cricket.

Jigs Club also had its own cricket team – according to the minutes of a club meeting on 1 January 1934, "it was decided to form a cricket club to play during the summer at Regents Park," and in May it was proposed that the club should sponsor a dance for the benefit of the International Cricket Club the following month. That summer they played against bandleader Harry Roy's XI, though minutes of the meeting stipulated that it had to be "members of the Musicians' Union only." A letter of welcome was again sent to the West Indian cricket team for their tour of 1939, during which *Calypso and Other West Indian Music*, presented by Johnson, was broadcast on BBC London regional service, immediately following the Lords Test match on 24 June. A regular at Jigs around this time was the Trinidadian trumpeter and younger brother of George, Cyril Blake, who recorded *Cyril's Blues* (Regal Zonophone MR 3597) with Laurence Caton on guitar, live at the club on 12 December 1941.

When Al Jennings travelled to Port of Spain in 1945 to recruit musicians for his Caribbean All-Star Orchestra, he returned to London with trumpeter Wilfred 'Pankey' Alleyne. Born in Mount Pleasant, Trinidad in 1916, his nickname was an abbreviation for 'Pancake,' a reference to his mother, a pastry maker. After her early death, he grew up in the Belmont orphanage, Port of Spain, where he learned to play the cornet. In his early 20s he played with Edmund Ross (later to become known as Edmundo Ros) and with a jazz-influenced band, The Moderneers, that included multi-instrumentalist Rupert Nurse and saxophonist Wally Stewart. They formed the nucleus of Jennings' All-Star Orchestra, an attempt to emulate Snakehips Johnson's band, which had suffered in the destruction at the Cafe de Paris in London during an air raid in 1941 and the resultant death of Johnson.

After several years playing in Europe, including a residency on the French Riviera and working in Mayfair clubs with pianist Clarie Wears and Tito Burns, Alleyne lost his job, as a result of his passion for cricket. After a game overran, he turned up late for a gig still in his whites to be told by the management, "Don't bother getting changed." He had played for the London West Indian Cricket Team as well as clarinettist and bandleader Sid Phillips' XI, and decided to follow the example of fellow Trinidadian Learie Constantine into professional club cricket, by joining Fleetwood in the Ribblesdale League, in 1950. According to *Wisden*, "he proved entertaining with bat, ball and (in the bar afterwards) trumpet." Heart trouble eventually forced him to give up the trumpet but he continued playing amateur cricket until he was 66.

Calypso was to gain great popularity in Britain, especially after West Indies' victory at Lords in 1950, although it acknowledged jazz in Lord Kitchener's *Kitch's Bebop Calypso*, (Melodisc 1162) which praises the new wave of black American jazz, mentioning Dizzy Gillespie, Charlie Parker and Miles Davis. Producer Denis Preston used a more varied musical combination from the usual calypso instrumentation, including the Jamaicans Bertie King (clarinet / alto-saxophone), Clinton Maxwell (drums), Freddy Grant (clarinet / tenor-saxophone), Neville Boucarut (string bass), Fitzroy Coleman (guitar) and the Guyanese pianist Mike McKenzie. Like Grant, both King and Maxwell had participated in the pre-war black music scene in London, the latter two having played together in Jamaica before migrating to Britain.

London during this period of the twentieth century was a meeting place for a large number of visitors who came to study, work and remain in the country, and organisations such as the League of Coloured People, as well as the numerous clubs that catered for Africans and Afro-Caribbeans, were where meetings could take place and links could be established.

One such person was Tunji Sowande. Born in Lagos, Nigeria in 1912, he trained as a chemist, but was a proficient singer and organist, drummer and saxophonist. In 1945, he decided to travel to the United Kingdom to pursue a career in Law, studying at King's College, London and Lincoln's Inn. Called to the Bar in 1952, he was offered a tenancy at Kings Bench Walk Chambers at the Inner Temple, London, a highly prestigious position not available to black barristers at the time. He had a black contemporary at the time, however, in the person of cricketer Learie Constantine. Sowande was a keen cricketer and member of the MCC.

He also took the opportunity to pursue his musical skills, performing with John Dankworth, Ronnie Scott, Ambrose Campbell and Edmundo Ros, as well as forming a long-standing partnership with the singer and pianist Rita Cann.

The story of his highly successful legal career, becoming the first black judge in Britain, was dramatised and performed in 2017 by Tayo Aluko in *Just An Ordinary Lawyer*. A show that interweaved politics, music and cricket, it hinges around the time in 1968 when Sowande became the first black head of a major barrister's chambers and takes in that year's conflicts in Africa, the assassinations of Martin Luther King and Robert Kennedy, the Black Power salute by Afro-American athletes John Carlos and Tommy Smith at the Mexico Olympics as well as the story of cricketer Basil D'Oliviera, who Sowande saw playing for England, and its political repercussions. The play described itself as musing on "Imperialism, Colonialism and Black people's struggle for freedom, justice and human rights, in Africa and the diaspora."

Tunji's elder brother was Fela Sowande who was born in 1905, also in Lagos, Nigeria, and who studied music, becoming a bandleader and playing jazz and popular early highlife music with the Chocolate Dandies and the Triumph Club Dance Band. He moved to London in 1934, initially to study civil engineering and supplement his income as a musician, but altered direction by studying European classical and popular music and playing in bands at clubs such as Frisco's, Chez Louis and the Old Florida. At this time London attracted many Caribbean and Africans. According to Marc Matera (*Black London – The Imperial Metropolis and Decoloniz-ation in the Twentieth Century*, 2015) Sowande and his wife were instrumental in persuading black Welsh guitarist Frank Deniz and his pianist wife, Clara to move from Cardiff to Camden Town. Sowande and Deniz were friends, going back to when they had worked together in New York, and Deniz and his brothers, Joe and Laurie, became regulars in the West End clubs. Also in London at that time was South African novelist Peter Abrahams, who wrote that Soho had the air and feel of a cosmopolitan village at the time, where "blacks congregated to eat and drink and pass the time and exchange news from 'home' at small nightclubs and little restaurants. This, looking back, was the seedbed of the later unity of African, American and Caribbean black folk." (Abrahams, *The Coyoba Chronicles*, 2000.) No doubt a regular topic of conversation would be cricket, particularly the visits of the West Indian team during this period, and connections were made through the League of Coloured People and the West African Students Union (WASU). Black musicians often got work through the Blake brothers, who recruited Caribbean and African talent during the 30s and 40s for the Cuba Club, the Shim Sham, The Nest (where Coleman Hawkins had visited in 1934), the Trade Winds, Havana Club, Blue Lagoon and others.

In 1936 Fela Sowande was solo pianist in a performance of George Gershwin's *Rhapsody in Blue* and also played as duo-pianist with Fats Waller. For a while he was theatre organist for the BBC, organist and choirmaster at Kingsway Hall, London and was pianist in the 1936 production of *Blackbirds*. In 1938 he took over from Ken Johnson at the Old Florida Club, with a new seven piece "All-coloured" group, and formed a professional partnership with singer Adelaide Hall, whose Trinidadian husband, Bert Hicks, ran the club. The following year he played organ in some recordings by the vocalist. During the Second World War he worked extensively for the BBC, but continued to compose, his works combining western and African music and he was known for incorporating African music into the European tradition, notably in his African Suite for Orchestra (1955). After some time in Nigeria, he moved to the USA to work at Howard University in Washington DC, the University of Pittsburgh and Kent State University.

4

Jazz and Cricket in the Colonies – South Africa and USA

Before the setting up of the United Cricket Board in 1991, cricket in South Africa was segregated into separate racial bodies and associations. Over the years, and in keeping with the apartheid system, only whites could play official test cricket and in 172 tests between 1888 and 1970 South Africa played against 'white' countries only – England, Australia and New Zealand. It was generally considered that cricket was outside the area of black South African culture, hardly ever played, as there were no records of it, but this was far from the truth, as Andre Odendaal's wonderfully comprehensive book *The Story of an African Game* (2003) shows. Notions that black people in South Africa had no culture of cricket were manifestly incorrect, and these assumptions were rooted in racism and apartheid, a perception based on prejudice and ignorance. Even the later, post-apartheid and relatively enlightened administrators of the game, such as John Passmore, admitted they didn't even realise blacks played cricket until the D'Oliviera affair blew up in 1968 and threatened the traditional structure of cricket in the country.

Odendaal's book chronicles the history of African (black) cricket going back to the late nineteenth century, especially in the Eastern Cape, which continued to the present day, despite the assault on social, political, economic and human rights throughout the twentieth century and the apartheid system set up in 1948.

As with other countries in the British Empire, cricket accompanied colonialism; in the Cape it was from when the British occupied in 1806, the first recorded match being in 1808. It started to be played in missionary schools in the 1850s, from which clubs and associations quickly grew. Victorian and imperial values were promoted, as in other countries of the Empire, as the white colonials controlled the official and recognised areas of the sport, often using it as a tool of authority and constraint. The process of assimilation and the breakdown and dispersion of Xhosa social structures went hand in hand with the attempt to anglicise the sons of Xhosa chiefs, in giving their children a British education. Governor Sir George Grey was instrumental in this and one such establishment was Bishop's Court in Cape Town, which later moved to Zonnebloem, on the edge of District Six. As well as academic subjects, students played sport, especially cricket, which was introduced at Zonnebloem College in 1861.

One student was Nathaniel Umhalla, who was later to study at St.Augustine's College in Canterbury, England, and who did much to promote the game for blacks in South Africa, both as player and as an administrator. In 1890 he helped found the South African Native Congress, later to develop into the African National Congress, and he became the first editor of the early independent black newspaper, *Izwi Labantu*, (*Voice of the People*).

During these early years, cricket was played by both blacks and whites and the standards were relatively even, reflected in the results of matches played between different race teams. However, there was the background of paternalism and control, though, as the authorities allowed these inter-race matches only on occasion or for special events. Cricket became increasingly popular, as ordinary people took an interest, not just those at schools and colleges, and for women as well as men.

The first cricket club in South Africa was founded in Port Elizabeth in 1859, where the first black club was also started ten years later. This was soon to be followed by Queenstown, in 1870, where a mixed team was set up. A good deal of interest was generated and many black clubs emerged, although criticism and questions arose as to why members of the indigenous population wanted to play the game of their oppressors, mimicking their colonial rulers. John Tengo Jabavu, editor of *Imvo Zabantsundu* (*Native Opinion*) suggested they "not only mean to persevere in playing at cricket, but are resolved to proceed from conquering to conquest so far as the cricket world is concerned." (3 November 1884)

The first English cricket side to tour was under Major R.G.Warton in 1888/9, with C. Aubrey Smith as captain, and despite attempts to set up an Anglo-African team that year, discrimination and segregation were the norms, for example at the Wanderers' ground, where a pavilion was built for Warton's tour, for whites only. There was no intention of relaxing barriers, power and privilege were maintained. Soon after this, the South African Cricket Association was founded, for whites only as a more rigid system of segregation grew.

Although the South African Coloured Cricket Board was set up in 1903, this fragmented into different boards and associations, partly due to the divisive governmental racial classifications that occurred, and black and coloured club cricket declined. However, it continued in local communities, and like music was indelibly linked to the social areas of life. During the 1920s and 30s this urban culture was known as 'marabi', in which dance parties or shabeens were the centre of community life, giving African working classes a new sense of identity. It was a time when African nationalist groups were also becoming more assertive.

Around 1934 The Bantu Sports Club in Johannesburg started to be more than a sports club, putting on musical events, including jazz evenings – on Sundays members could listen and dance to "radiogram music" on the club verandah. Many social facilities were at the nearby Bantu Men's Social Centre, where political activist Walter and Albertina Sisulu had their wedding in the early 40s, the music provided by the Merry Blackbirds Jazz Band. The guests included Nelson Mandela, with whom Walter Sisulu was later imprisoned on Robben Island.

Jazz had arrived in South Africa, initially through the influence of African-American minstrels and ragtime pianists who visited from the 1890s onwards. This, with gospel and spirituals, was adapted and mixed with traditional forms, including marabi music. Inspiration also came from listening to American musicians on record – Louis Armstrong, New Orleans jazz and dance bands, then later Duke Ellington, Count Basie and others, as well as from American films.

During the 1920s Queenstown became known as 'Little Jazz Town' because of the many bands that played there, such as Meekly Matshikizi's Blue Rhythm Syncopators and William Mbali's Big Four. The Merry Blackbirds were one of the many bands that arose. Founded in 1930, they originally comprised of two violins, trombone, piano and drums, and were called Motsieloa's Band, after Griffiths Motsieloa and his wife Emily. It changed name in 1932 and changed its line-up, being led by alto saxophonist Peter Rezant. It had Enoch Matunjwa (trumpet), Philip Mbanjwa (alto, trombone), Mac Modikwe (tenor sax), Emily Motsieloa (piano), Ike Shaping (violin), Fats Dunjwa (bass) and Tommy Koza (drums). They mainly imitated American dance bands, but were a leading outfit at the time. It also featured vocalist Marjorie Pretorius, South Africa's first black female jazz singer, who continued into the 1960s.

Jazz bands sprang up in most of the cities. In Johannesburg the leading bands were the Harlem Swingsters, the Alexandra All Stars and the Jazz Maniacs, founded by Doorfontein shabeen pianist and saxophonist Solomon 'Zulu Boy' Cele, and including reedman Wilson 'King Force' Silgee, described by Johannesburg newspaper the *Sun Times* as "playing a clarinet that sounded like a snake charmer's flute."

Other bands included the Gay Gaieties, the Synco Fans and the Pitch Black Follies, many of whom fronted their bands with female vocalists – Dolly Rathebe, Dorothy Masuku and Miriam Makeba making their names in this way. Through these bands the spirit of marabi was taken to the dance halls and inspired individual jazz musicians, such as trumpeters Elijah Nkwanyana and Hugh Masekela, saxophonist Kippie Moeketsi, trombonist Jonas Gwangwa, pianist Dollar Brand (Abdullah Ibrahim) and many more.

A number found their way to Europe, living in exile and estranged from their mother country and its draconian government. Those who settled in Britain included Chris McGregor, Dudu Pukwana, Louis Moholo and Mongezi Feza, who formed the Blue Notes. Manfred Mann and his friend, bassist Harry Miller also came in the early 60s, Miller becoming a well-known and respected figure on the London scene, playing with fellow South Africans, European and local musicians and setting up Ogun Records with his wife, Hazel Miller. He was a keen cricket fan who enjoyed visiting games and would often be in conversation about it to fellow enthusiasts such as trumpeter Harry Beckett, saxophonist Elton Dean and drummer Pip Pyle. Dean and Pyle also played for an informal cricket team known as 'The Rotters'.

One of the most famous African cricket clubs was New Brighton. Founded in 1917, it rose to prominence and by the 1950s was a major force in black club cricket, when it included Eric Majola, a member of a famous cricketing family. Team mate and fellow opening bowler was Lent Maqoma, a member of the Xhosa royal family and who was described in *African Sports* (1953) as a "powerful and polished hard-hitter," He was named by the magazine as one of the 'Big Four' of Eastern Province cricket, with Majola, Matthews Mokonenyane and Chinky Mgubela. According to

Eastern Province 'Big Four' 1954: Lent Maqoma, Eric Majola, Matthews Mokonenyane and Chinky Mgubela, *courtesy Andre Odendaal Collection*

Andre Odendaal, Maqoma was also a gifted saxophonist, who became the first principal of the Johnson Marwanqa School.

Maqoma was also to play tenor sax in Myer Kaplan's musical production, *Shanty Town Revue*, which according to journalist Jimmy Matyu in his *About Town* column for *The Herald* was Port Elizabeth's first all-African musical revue and an answer to *King Kong*, Alfred Herbert's African Jazz and Variety stage musical. Other band members included trumpeter Kekie Njikelana, who also acted, and trombonist Mike Ngxokolo. Writing in 2006 about music in Port Elizabeth in the 1950s and 60s, Matyu described *Shanty Town Revue* as "vibrant and exhilarating, but with a weak plot. It opened to a packed Crispin Hall in Mount Road on a special permit as all-African shows were not allowed by the Reservations Separate Amenities Act to perform in white suburbs. Later with some funding from the (Xhosa newspaper) *Imvo Zabantsundu* management, as social editor I invited them to come over to Zwelitsha. This was when I made a fool out of apartheid by managing to get the Town Hall in King William's Town, which had been a citadel of apartheid and out of bounds to blacks."

Maqoma was later to embark on a controversial career in the government of the Ciskei homeland.

America is the birthplace of jazz. As baseball is the major bat/ball sport, there is the perception that cricket has had no place in the history of the United States. However, this is not the case.

There is evidence of cricket in the pre-Revolutionary era, played by British colonists, by the start of the eighteenth century, but this appears to be informal. In a diary he kept between 1709 and 1712, William Byrd, owner of the Virginia plantation Westover, noted

> I rose at 6 o'clock and read a chapter in Hebrew. About 10 o'clock Dr. Blair, and Major
> and Captain Harrison came to see us. After I had given them a glass of sack we played
> cricket. I ate boiled beef for my dinner. Then we played at shooting with arrows... and
> went to cricket again till dark. (Simon Worrall, *Smithsonian Magazine*, Oct 2006)

There are references to it in Georgia around 1737 – a New York newspaper from 1739 contained an advertisement for cricket players and the first documented competition, reported in the *New York Gazette* and the *Weekly Post Boy*, occurred in 1751 in Manhattan. The rules of the game were formalised in 1754, apparently by Benjamin Franklin when he brought a copy of the 1744 *Laws of Cricket* back from England. By 1779 cricket clubs started appearing, notably Brooklyn and Greenwich, and in 1795 at Richmond, Virginia. Much was identifiably English, mainly soldiers and expatriates. By the end of the eighteenth century and into the nineteenth century it had appeared at educational establishments such as Harvard, Dartmouth and Yale. Legend has it that George Washington's troops played what they called "wickets" at Valley Forge in the summer of 1778. After the Revolution, a 1786 advertisement for cricket equipment appeared in the *New York Independent Journal*, and newspaper reports of that time frequently mention "young gentlemen" and "men of fashion" taking up the sport.

In 1838 a match was played between English residents from Sheffield and Nottingham, for wager of 100 dollars, near the Ferry House Tavern, Brooklyn, which started a series of matches for money in Brooklyn. 1840 saw contact between American and Canadian teams, when the St George Club of New York played Toronto.

New York Cricket Club was founded in October 1843 followed by Chicago in 1840, and by 1845 in Rochester, Cincinnati, Natchez (Mississippi), Syracuse and Macon (Georgia). It was also played on a larger scale in Philadelphia, the home of a sizable population of immigrant English mill workers. At this time, both baseball and cricket were popular, reflecting the growing interest in organised and participant sports and the change in the social and urban environment of the antebellum period. There was a fair amount of contact between the two. Many players played both and Union Star CC in New York shared their ground with Brooklyn Baseball Club and had overlapping membership.

Tom Melville, in his book *The Tented Field – A History of Cricket in America* (1998), suggests there was also was a need for a national game at this time, free from foreign influences, as the country became more sensitive to its national image and prestige. By 1857, antebellum cricket reached its peak, and the idea arose of inviting England's best cricketers over, although according to Melville, it was probably initiated by English cricket authorities. In 1859 a squad captained by Nottinghamshire batsman George Parr, and including John Wisden, came and played in New York and Philadelphia. This resulted in renewed interest in the game generally and the appearance of new clubs, together with greater participation in schools and colleges, but it was heavily dependent on the immigrant English population and was unsuccessful in attracting Americans, possibly apart from Philadelphia.

Further links between cricket and baseball sprung up, but with the outbreak of the Civil War in 1861, all games were suspended as the country went into turmoil. There was a steep decline after the War, but a sharp increase in baseball, in which there was a huge sudden interest. This has been seen as possibly result of pressure to establish a national game, in the name of patriotism, but also the view that cricket was too slow and drawn out, and too English. Baseball was faster, easier to learn and needed little in the way of equipment. Soon baseball came to the ascendancy; by the early 1870s, there were 2,000 baseball clubs, 100,000 players, 250,000 spectators and, perhaps most important, a sound commercial structure.

But cricket was still popular: in 1878, around 15,000 people in Philadelphia watched a local eleven hold the Australians, already emerging as a strong cricketing force, to a draw, and fifteen years later, Philadelphia beat the Aussies. There developed a class element – cricket started to be regarded as having a social position apart from the mass interest of baseball, attracting the middle and upper classes – greater respectability – and not answerable to market forces. It became more aligned to the leisure classes who had finances and free time. Its negative reputation as being less exciting became a positive element in it being free from over-excitement and rowdiness of baseball. Although working class cricket also revived in the post war period - the industrial areas of the east coast had factory and mining teams, and several women's teams were set up – it started to disappear when the immigrant communities who played it, as an expression of their ethnic identity, started to be absorbed in the local American culture or became dispersed by moving on.

During the post-war period there were visits from Irish and West Indian teams. Melville's view is that "Britain's traditionally progressive racial policies within its colonies enabled late nineteenth century American cricket to generally avoid the taint of racial prejudice that plagued so many other American sports during this period." This is all relative of course.

> Blacks are known to have played cricket in New Orleans and Philadelphia as early as the 1860s, though any effort to arrange interracial play during this racially charged period of American history was as strongly opposed as any other attempt to bring about closer racial contacts. (Melville)

In the report of one attempt in Washington, Pennsylvania, in 1869, the local press strongly objected. It was most popular with black Americans of West Indian descent, who were immigrating to the larger east coast urban areas. Playing cricket reinforced its cultural identity and New York's first West Indian cricket club was founded in 1893, having been initially supported by the West Indian Benevolent & Social League. By the turn of the century at least a dozen other West Indian clubs were active in the New York area. There were instances of inter-racial cricket around this time – the Portland Cricket Club in Oregon played an integrated team of British sailors during their shore leave in 1901 and the Philadelphia Club that toured Jamaica in 1909 played several games against local black teams. "Even George Wright, despite a long career in unofficially segregated baseball, felt no compunction in urging West Indian George F. Samuels in 1892 to organize a West Indian cricket team and enter it into competition with other Boston area clubs." (Melville)

Wright and his brother Samuel were eminent figures in both cricket and baseball during the late nineteenth century; George captaining a side that played Lord Hawke's touring team in 1891. Other tours included that of Pelham Warner in 1898 and Ranjitsinhji's in 1899. In 1903 there was a successful tour of England by Philadelphia which included a draw against Oxford and wins against both Gloucestershire and Nottinghamshire.

During the late years of the nineteenth century, interest in cricket declined further. One explanation, which Melville supports, was that of Melvin Adelman (*A Sporting Time: New York City and the Rise of Modern Athletics 1820-70*, 1986) who put it down as the interplay between culturally controlled behaviour and its expression through specific sporting structures:

> Baseball, with its shorter, rapid transition structure, and alternating periods of excitement and dramatic pauses, provided Americans with a cultural expression that cricket, at least within its traditional structural limitations, couldn't duplicate. Cricket failed in America because it never established an American character. (Melville)

In short, there was a cultural resistance to the game.

The early years of the twentieth century saw a rapid decline in cricket although there were slight signs of resurgence through immigrant communities from South Asia and the West Indies. In 1932 the actor C. Aubrey Smith established the Hollywood Cricket Club, which included Boris Karloff, and in the sixties, the USA Cricket Association was formed, later becoming an associate member of the ICC.

There have been American players that have stood out and would have had success in any cricket team: George Patterson, J Barton (Bart) King, and John Lester. Boston-born Ken Weekes played for the West Indies on their tour of England in 1939, scoring 137 at The Oval in the Test match, and more recently there has been Jehan Mubarak, Washington DC-born, who made his test debut for Sri Lanka in 2002, and whose batting was described by fellow player Ranjit Fernando as "poetry in motion."

Jamaican Desmond Lewis is worth a mention; a wicketkeeper who played in 3 tests in 1971 for the West Indies against India. He scored 81 in a stand of 84 with Lance Gibbs and 88 in a partnership of 166 with Rohan Kanhai, and continued to play for Jamaica until 1976, after which he moved to Atlanta, Georgia, successfully coaching at the Tropical Sports Club. "When I came here, you couldn't find 11 people to make a team," Lewis said, "now we have 23 teams in the Atlanta region, with about 400 players actively involved."

In social contrast to the affluent cricketing circles, there has also been the interesting Compton Cricket Club, in Los Angeles, which includes Latino and African American ex-gang members. Founded in 1995 by homeless activist Ted Hayes and film producer Katy Haber, its aims have been to combat the negative effects of local poverty, urban decay and crime, and help players develop respect, self-esteem and self-discipline. It has toured Australia and the UK, at one point meeting the late MP Mo Mowlam at Stormont Castle and presenting Gerry Adams with a cricket bat and David Pringle with a hurling stick, to help the peace accord. In 2001 Brian Lara guested for them in a game and in 2003, Warwickshire cricketer Paul Smith helped train them as part of his work with Cricket Without Boundaries, a charity that seeks to empower communities through cricket.

There are few examples of crossover between cricket and jazz in the USA, a contributing factor possibly being the decline of interest in the sport taking place before the rise of jazz, apart from isolated cases – saxophonist Spike Robinson being one, and the connection of musicians with band leader and agent Vic Lewis. One cricketer who moved to the US and made a name for himself is Orlando Le Fleming – however, this was in the world of jazz. According to his website, bassist Orlando Le Fleming's "facility as an improviser and capacity as a team player were honed not on the bandstand, nor in the practice room, but on the cricket pitch."

Le Fleming was born in Birmingham (UK) in 1976, moved to Exeter and made his cricketing debut for Devon in the 1992 Minor Counties Championship against Cheshire. He played 24 times for them, until 1996, as a right-handed batsman and medium-pace bowler. He also played in the NatWest Trophy, against Yorkshire in 1994, taking the wickets of Paul Grayson and wicketkeeper Richard Blakey, and against Essex in 1996. In addition, he played eight 2nd XI Championship matches for Somerset 2nd XI in 1995.

After retiring from cricket, he followed his other great interest, as a bass player, performing with many names on the British jazz scene. These included Jason

Rebello, Tommy Smith, Roger Beaujolais and Guy Barker. He moved to America in 2003 and is now a highly regarded musician in New York, having worked with Branford Marsalis, Billy Cobham, Jimmy Cobb and others, and leading his own band, whose 2013 album *Owl Trio* (with guitarist Lage Lund and saxophonist Will Vinson) was reviewed in *Downbeat* magazine: "Everything about this album, which should contend for debut of the year honours, is a resounding success. The music swings effortlessly, every utterance is gorgeous and the recording is intimate and beautiful."

In 2019 Le Fleming generously responded to questions:

Where were you brought up/educated and did you play at school/ for a club before going into county cricket?

In Exeter and went to Exeter Cathedral School and then Exeter School.

I played for school teams and Devon/ West of England/ England youth teams but most importantly I played men's cricket for Exeter CC, in the first team when I was 14 then that led to me playing for Devon CC when I was 15. My father built a cricket net in our garden and would also take me up to Taunton to practice with coaches Dennis Breakwell and Peter Robinson regularly.

Which cricketers particularly inspired you?

I used to watch Somerset when they had Botham, Richards and Garner! Also my older brother Felix was a lovely batsman who played to a very good standard too.

Is there a game you played in that you have particular memories of?

Playing against Yorkshire (Gough, Richardson, Vaughan) in the Nat West trophy was fun, we gave them a good game and I bowled well. I once dismissed Alvin Kallicharran in a Minor Counties game and he said well bowled as he walked passed me, that was pretty memorable. Winning the Minor Counties Trophy at Lords was special. Devon was an unstoppable team then, largely thanks to Peter Roebuck.

When did you start to listen to jazz and play and who was instrumental in your development in the music?

I started out on violin, my parents are classical musicians and huge influences. I then discovered the bass guitar through Level 42 and Mark King (via my older brother) when I was about 10. My father took me to see Dill Katz who recommended Weather Report, Miles Davis etc and also I had a great teacher at school called Dave Bowen who hipped me to a lot of jazz and fusion. I took up the upright bass when I was 19 and focused on a lot more traditional jazz, thanks to local piano player Craig Milverton, who was also a big influence early on.

Did you play locally when a student in London? Who with?

All the guys in the year above me at the Royal Academy of Music were great – the Fishwicks (Steve and Matt), Gareth Lockrane, Tom Cawley – so I played with them.

By the third year I was also touring the country and playing a bit with Jason Rebello and Julian Joseph who were my early mentors. I used to play a lot at the 606 and Ronnie's too.

Do you think there was any connection between the way you played cricket and your approach to playing music?

I think the discipline of playing a sport helped me organize my practice and achieve results pretty quickly. I think also performing under pressure in sport helped me deal with similar situations in music and made me a bit more thick skinned and relaxed in musical situations, where the stakes are less black and white and severe. I try and be supportive and a team player. Sometimes I play looking to get that same buzz I got from sport and sometimes that's too much for the music and sometimes just right, depending on the players, the compositions etc.

5

Mr. Showbiz : Vic Lewis

The bandleader Vic Lewis was regarded by some for his braggadocio – but his stories often turned out to be true. Born in Brent in 1919, his father, who played for Kent 2nd team and the Royal Flying Corps in the First World War, gave his son an interest from an early age. "He was a slow left-arm bowler," Lewis told Brian Johnston (*View From The Boundary*, BBC Radio, at Old Trafford 11 August 1990), "I have two or three balls at home which I treasure very much. 'Nine for forty-six' was one particular one and there was one 'eight for twenty-seven', polished and with little plaques on them." Lewis and his brother held bats or balls in their hands "while other children stared at their rattles or sucked their dummies" he recalled. By his teenage years, however, he decided on a career in music, as he had developed an interest in jazz guitar, particularly after hearing records by Eddie Condon and Eddie Lang.

After forming his Swing String Quartet in 1935, which was based on the music of Joe Venuti and Eddie Lang, he worked with George Shearing, Carlo Krahmer and even Django Reinhardt and Stephane Grappelli on one of their London visits. Then he visited New York and stayed with Leonard Feather, who he knew from the No.1 Rhythm Club in London. Through Feather he met and played with Joe Marsala, Buddy Rich and Joe Bushkin at the Hickory House, as well as guesting at clubs with Pee Wee Russell, George Wettling, Sidney Bechet, Zutty Singleton and Wellman Braud, and sitting in with Tommy Dorsey, Jack Teagarden and Louis Armstrong.

He spent the war years in the RAF, where he met drummer Jack Parnell and saxophonist Buddy Featherstonhaugh and formed the Radio Rhythm Club Sextet, broadcasting on BBC Radio. During this time, he played cricket for Bomber Command against a team from RAF Upper Heyford, which was captained by Squadron Leader Bill Edrich, of Middlesex and England fame, and who was a *Wisden Cricketer of the Year* in 1940. From 1944 to 1946 Lewis and Jack Parnell formed a band, making several recordings, then, inspired by the music of Stan Kenton, came the Vic Lewis Orchestra, which played at the Paris Festival of Jazz in 1949 on the same bill as Dizzy Gillespie, Charlie Parker and Miles Davis. The band included Kathy Stobart, Ronnie Chamberlain and Hank Shaw. Heavily influenced by Kenton and Gerry Mulligan, he recorded *Music for Moderns* in 1950 and employed many of the young British musicians during that decade. On the album *Mulligan's Music* (1954) arrangements were adhered to, but soloists given the opportunity to express themselves, notably trombonist Johnny Watson and the young Tubby Hayes, whose baritone solo on *Bark For Barksdale* is an indication of things to come, when he would build solos like a batsman compiling an extended innings.

Lewis also founded the Vic Lewis Cricket Club, which featured showbiz celebrities and cricketers and raised money for several charities. He wrote quite extensively about his career and successes in his book *Music & Maiden Overs* (1987), described by one writer as "an embarrassingly self-regarding volume." When Lewis took American arranger, composer and bandleader Nelson Riddle and his son Christopher to Lords, "while I left them briefly to go for a tinkle, a local youngster walked up to Nelson and said, 'Excuse me, but was that really the famous Vic Lewis you were with just before?'"

Over the years his cricket team included many notable cricketers – Gary Sobers, Rohan Kanhai, Fred Trueman, Brian Statham, Ken Barrington, John Snow, Rodney Marsh, Hanif Mohammad and others would find themselves playing with the likes of Elton John, David Frost, Tom Baker, Michael Parkinson, Oliver Reed, George Best, John Dankworth, Peter Cook and many more. The book shows photos of Lewis hitting a square drive off the bowling of Norman Gifford in a benefit match for Glenn Turner at Worcester in 1976, opening the batting with V.L. Manjrekar at Oldham in 1958 and with Frank Worrell at Rochdale in 1955, during which the pair put on 74 for the first wicket, although Lewis' contribution was more modest than his illustrious partner: Worrell 64, Lewis 10. A regular in his celebrity team was TV chat-show host, broadcaster and journalist Michael Parkinson, an ardent follower of Yorkshire cricket and who had an early interest in traditional jazz, especially Jelly Roll Morton and the Armstrong Hot Fives. As a youngster he wrote an article comparing Gloucestershire, Worcestershire and England cricketer Tom Graveney with clarinettist Johnny Dodds: "I thought they were the two great stylists of all time," he recalled in an interview in *Jazz at Ronnie Scott's* magazine. Parkinson was to extend his interest to the big bands of Basie, Ellington, Herman and Kenton before moving towards modern jazz. One of Lewis' sides that played against the jazz team, the Ravers Cricket Club, included comedian Bernard Bresslaw, entertainer Roy Castle, singer Ronnie Carroll and DJ Pete Murray.

As an agent and manager, Lewis was known to take visiting artists to matches –a photo in *Music & Maiden Overs* shows Gerry Mulligan and actress Sandy Dennis at Mill Hill cricket ground. On another occasion he took Nat King Cole to watch a test match at Lord's. The singer enjoyed himself so much he stayed all day, ending up on the players' balcony and being presented with a cricket ball by Frank Worrell, the West Indian captain, as a memento of the visit. He also took cricketers out to West End clubs. In the late 50s he was engaged in booking singers for the Blue Lagoon in Carnaby Street, which included Helen Merrill, Abbey Lincoln and Dinah Washington. According to Lewis, on one night in 1959 he had arranged to meet West Indian cricketers Gary Sobers, Collie Smith and Tom Dewdney there as they were driving from the north of England to play in a charity game the following day. They never arrived, having crashed into a cattle truck near Stone in Staffordshire which resulted in the tragic death of Collie Smith.

Lewis was also musical director for *The Ashes Song*, sung by Ray Illingworth's victorious MCC team than beat Australia in 1970/1. The reverse side was a version of *Hello Dolly* but with a new verse ending, "The Ashes won't ever go away again." Optimistically, as they were to lose them in 1974/5.

A keen collector of cricket club ties, Lewis wrote *Cricket Ties – an International Guide for Cricket Lovers* (1984).

6

The Ravers

Vic Lewis' showbiz team played against one of the more curious teams that emerged at that time – the Ravers C.C. Founded in 1954 in the Blue Posts pub, as a result of Wally Fawkes and George Webb deciding that the 100 Club (then known as the Lyttelton Club) should have a jazz cricket team, its early members included Mick Mulligan, Max Jones, Sandy Brown, Jim Bray, Harry Hayes, Monty Sunshine and agent Lyn Dutton. During the next few years Welsh trumpeter Albert (Alwyn) Hall, Bruce Turner, Frank Parr, Frank Holder and his brother Ovid, Bob Dawbarn, Jim Godbolt and Ray Smith were all regulars. Others in the jazz fraternity that later played included Brian Lemon, John Chilton, Johnny Barnes, Campbell Burnap, Jeff Horton of the 100 Club, writer and former editor of *Melody Maker* Richard Williams (described by Godbolt as a "penetrating fast bowler"), the actor (and active campaigner for racial equality) Louis Mahoney, Richie Bryant, Tim Prowse and Martin Ash (aka Sam Spoons of the Bonzo Dog Band).

That a cricket team should be made up of those involved in jazz should come as no surprise. As Spike Hughes in *The Art of Coarse Cricket* pointed out, amateur teams are largely dependent for their existence on an attitude of mind, far more common in England than the casual student of cricket might think. He found it in colleges, the forces, the BBC, and "in the variety profession, on the legitimate stage, among dance band musicians, in film studios, the Territorial Army, the editorial staffs of newspapers, in the London Philharmonic Orchestra... even among the publicity men of Wardour Street."

In the history of the Ravers, Frank Parr was the most eminent cricketer, having played for Lancashire from 1951-54 and tipped by *The Times* as a potential future England wicket keeper. Herbert Strudwick, England wicketkeeper in the 1920s thought he was very special. Born in Wallasey in 1928, he played trombone with the Merseysippi Jazz Band from 1949 and was seen as something of an oddity, apparently based on his scruffiness and habit of holding jam sessions in the changing room. The Lancashire and England fast bowler, Brian Statham, described Frank as "a fine wicketkeeper, but he was an arty, untidy type who looked what he was, a spare-time musician. Even in flannels, walking on to the field, he still managed to look anything but a cricketer." As long as the easy-going Nigel Howard was captain of Lancashire, Frank's eccentricities weren't a problem, but in 1954, the more formal Cyril Washbrook took over and Frank was soon dropped. According to Stephen Chalke in his obituary (*Independent* 16 May 2012): "On one occasion, at Oxford, Parr played his trombone in the dressing room, with a team mate beating time with

Jazz at the Savoy, Fred Elizalde Orchestra including Maurice Allom, 1927

Spike Hughes and his All American Orchestra, 1933

Nocturne; Someone Stole Gabriel's Horn; Pastorale; Bugle Horn Rag; Arabesque; Fanfare; Sweet Sorrow Blues; Music at Midnight; Sweet Sue, Just You; Air in D-Flat; Donegal Cradle Song; Firebird; Music at Sunrise; How Come You Do Me Like You Do?

Shad Collins, Leonard Davis, Bill Dillard, Henry Red Allen, Howard Scott (tp); Dickie Wells, Wilbur de Paris, George Washington (tb); Benny Carter, Wayman Carver, Howard Johnson (cl,as); Coleman Hawkins (cl,ts); Chu Berry (ts); Red Rodriguez, Luis Russell (p); Lawrence Lucie (gtr); Ernest Hill (b); Kaiser Marshall or Sid Catlett (d); Spike Hughes (b, dir,arr). New York, April 18, May 18, 19, 1933.

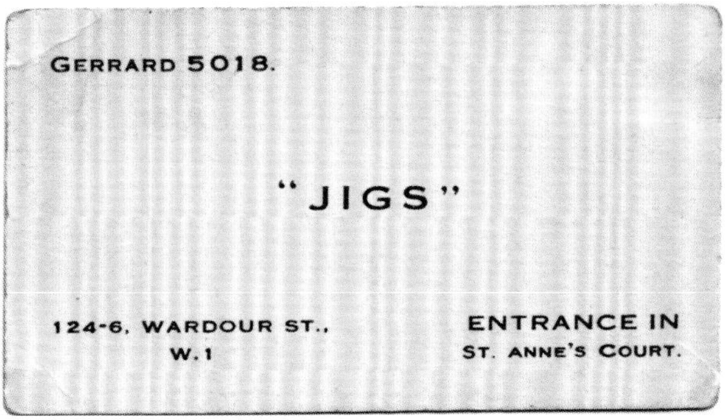

GERRARD 5018.

"JIGS"

124-6, WARDOUR ST.,
W.1

ENTRANCE IN
ST. ANNE'S COURT.

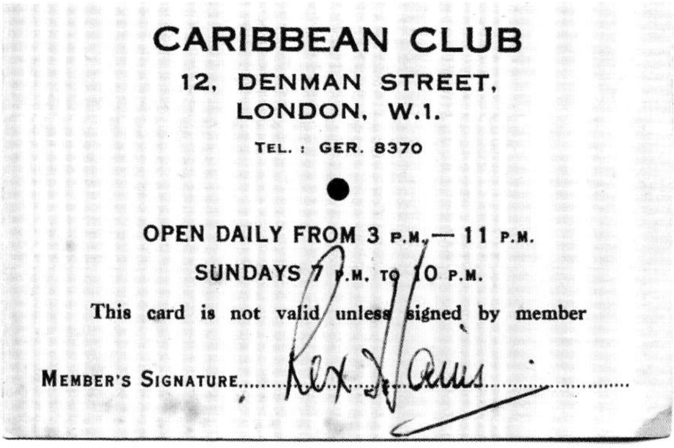

CARIBBEAN CLUB

12, DENMAN STREET,
LONDON, W.1.

TEL. : GER. 8370

●

OPEN DAILY FROM 3 P.M. — 11 P.M.
SUNDAYS 7 P.M. TO 10 P.M.

This card is not valid unless signed by member

MEMBER'S SIGNATURE......*Rex J. Harris*......

MEMBERSHIP CARD

Coloured Peoples Club

23, FRITH STREET,
LONDON, W.1

This card must be produced at the door,
otherwise admission will be refused,

Membership cards

Wilfred 'Pankey' Alleyne. *Photo © Valerie Wilmer Collection*

Orlando Le Fleming bowling for Somerset.
Permission of Orlando Le Fleming

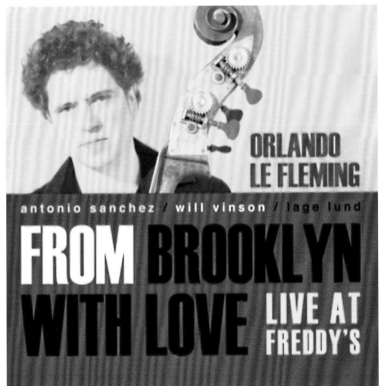

From Brooklyn With
Love. *Permission of
Orlando Le Fleming*

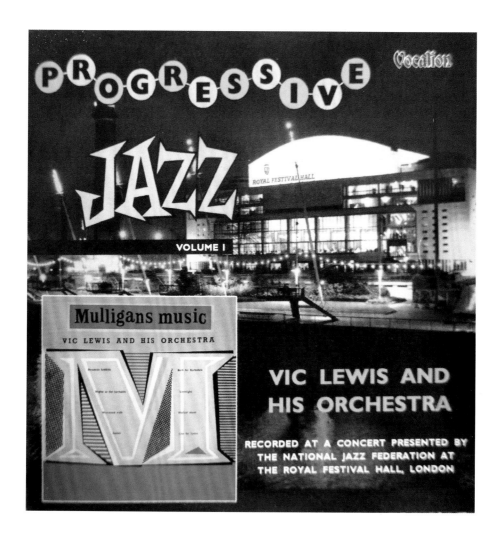

Vic Lewis and His Orchestra. Mulligan's Music/Progressive Jazz, 1954-6

MCC Ashes Team/Vic Lewis single, 1971

Jazz at the Flamingo featuring Tubby Hayes, 1956

Ravers' 50th year cap

Just not Cricket! *Courtesy Steve Beresford*

Lancashire 1953. Brian Statham back row centre, Frank Parr to his left

a stump; 'Much to Washy's disgust.' Washbrook's vitriolic words, on the racial origins of jazz music, were never forgotten."

During a period in the Second XI he was offered a job with Worcestershire, but this was scuppered by Washbrook writing to them advising against it, saying "I should inform you that he can be a grave social risk." His days as a professional cricketer were over and the rejection hit him hard. "I thought it was the end of the world," he later said, "it's probably why I took up serious drinking." He had played 48 first class matches for Lancashire and one for the MCC, was close to being selected for the 1953 tour of the West Indies, scored 508 runs in total with a highest score of 42 and took 69 catches and 20 stumpings. (See appendix for career statistics)

In 1956 he joined Mick Mulligan's Magnolia Jazz Band, fronted by singer George Melly, a period well documented in Melly's book *Owning Up* (1965). "All jazzmen are kicking against something," Frank said, "and it comes out when they blow. If they knew what they were kicking against, they wouldn't blow nearly so well."

Melly described Frank graphically in the book – his untidiness, lack of personal hygiene, even the dramatic speed with which he would pass through the stages of drunkenness: "wild humour, self-pity and unconsciousness, all well-seasoned with the famous Parr grimaces."

Early Ravers, circa 1955. L-R) Peter Hughes, Micky Ashman, Jim Bray, Sandy Brown, Mick Mulligan, Chris Curtis, Bert Bowd, Barry Kent, George McCallum, Elmer Smith; (Seated) Doug Calderwood, Lyn Dutton, Wally Fawkes

His actual fall had a monumental simplicity. One moment he was perpendicular, the next horizontal. "The only warning we had of his collapse was that, just before it happened, Frank announced that he was 'only fit for the human scrap heap' and this allowed us time to move any glasses, tables, chairs or instruments out of the way."

He explained why Parr's time as a promising wicketkeeper was short-lived. The professional cricketer, Melly observed, "is expected to behave within certain defined limits. He can be a 'rough diamond', even 'a bit of a character', but he must know his place. If he smells of sweat, it must be fresh sweat. He must dress neatly and acceptably. His drinking must be under control. He must know when to say 'sir'."

However, Frank had none of these attributes: "He was an extreme social risk, a complicated rebel whose world swarmed with demons and Jack O'Lanterns", and he "concealed a formidable and well-read intelligence behind a stylised oafishness".

Chairman:
GEORGE WEBB

Treasurer:
RAY SMITH

Captain:
FRANK PARR

Vice-Captain:
ROBIN RATHBORNE

MEMBERS ARE ASKED TO
ADHERE STRICTLY TO THE
PROCEDURE REGARDING
AVAILABILITY AND SELECTION
AND TO ARRIVE AT THE
GROUND IN GOOD TIME.

PROMPT PAYMENT OF YOUR
SUBSCRIPTION WOULD BE
APPRECIATED.

RAVERS C. C.
Affiliated to C. C. C.

President:
LYN DUTTON

Hon. Match Secretaries:
BOB DAWBARN
TEM. 2468 Ex. 507 (Day)
PRI. 0752 (Night)

MAX JONES
TEM. 2468 (Day)
PRI. 7363 (Night)
both of
26 Primrose Hill Road, N.W.3

Fixture Secretary:
JIM GODBOLT
9 Shaftesbury Mews,
Stratford Rd., W.8
WES. 0052/3

**A ROVING XI COMPRISED OF
PERSONALITIES IN JAZZ**

Ravers fixture card 1960 season

His fellow band members, Melly recalled, never knew the reason for Parr's quarrel with the captain of Lancashire which ended his cricketing career, "but after a month or two in his company we realised it must have been inevitable".

Melly described him as extremely limited in what he would eat: "Fried food, especially bacon and eggs, headed the list"; food such as soup or cheese came under the heading of "pretentious bollocks". Although Frank liked certain food, "his attitude was decidedly odd," wrote Melly. "He would crouch over his plate, knife and fork at the ready in his clenched fists, and glare down at the harmless egg and inoffensive bacon, enunciating, as though it were part of some barbarous and sadistic ritual, the words 'I'll murder it'. What followed, a mixture of jabbing, tearing, stuffing, grinding and gulping, was a distressing spectacle."

Despite his eccentricities, Frank insisted that he was the only 'normal' member of the band. As a result, any exceptionally dissipated behaviour would provoke the bandleader Mick Mulligan to say: "Hello, Frank. Feeling normal then?"

In the 1950s the Mulligan band became synonymous with a jazz lifestyle that involved drinking copious amounts of alcohol and engaging in wild behaviour, sexual and otherwise, at all hours of the day and night, vividly described in Melly's *Owning Up*. Inevitably the band's performances were often affected, sometimes disastrously - on one occasion, when playing solo trumpet, Mulligan was so drunk that all he could do was blow hard and very loudly, producing 32 bars of ear-shattering cacophony.

From the evidence of the few recording made, however, the band could play well, Frank in particular, but by the end of the fifties their style of revivalist "trad" jazz was going out of fashion. "(We) knew something was up when we did a concert with Tommy Steele," George Melly recalled later. "We did our set and the audience was quieter than usual. Then Tommy Steele came on and these small girls exploded into shrieks. Our trombonist, Frank Parr – famously depressive – said we would all be on the breadline."

Mulligan's band wound up in 1961 and after a short spell with the Clyde Valley Stompers, Frank put away his trombone. In 1969 Frank met Christine Dunbar, who acted under her stage name of Sarah Maddern, at the Capricorn club in Soho, and soon moved in with her and her family. By then he was Acker Bilk's manager, after which he worked for a company that sold advertising space for charities whilst continuing to play for the Ravers until the early 90s. He also took jobs as a film extra, appearing briefly in *Psychoville* (2009) and *The King's Speech* (2010). He died in 2012, aged 83.

The team had its share of eccentrics – *Melody Maker* photographer Eric Jelly often unsettled opposing batsmen, as when fielding, the ball would make a deafening clank that resounded around the ground after hitting his metal leg support. George Webb bowled leg breaks and if he failed to take a wicket tried to scowl the batsman out. According to Jim Godbolt, Wally Fawkes was an elegant batsman, a medium fast bowler but a sluggardly fieldsman. When he later left the side he claimed that "his left leg coming heavily down the popping crease was making it progressively shorter and he would have to retire before it disappeared entirely."

When captain Lyn Dutton asked Bruce Turner to field at square leg, the saxophonist was reluctant and when pressed for a reason answered "don't like going anywhere that's square, Dad." He was in the habit of calling anyone "Dad" although it was said that when in the company of his father, was unsure how to address him. As a child, Turner moved around quite a lot, due to the work of his father, a college professor, including some time in India. It was there he saw the MCC touring team, playing against Hyderabad State. The match was followed by a dinner in honour of the visiting team. "There I was, in a room of cricketing legends, taking in every word and gesture of the great players. (Hedley) Verity and (Fred) Bakewell devoured their meal in silence, but (Stan) Nichols and Ken Farnes talked cricket all the way through dinner and at one point even used the salt and pepper pots to demonstrate a fielding manoeuvre," recalled Turner (*Hot Air, Cool Music* 1984). He was also introduced to

The Ravers c.1957/58:
Back row L-R: Pete Appleby, Bob Dawbarn, Jim Bray, Jim Godbolt, Mick Mulligan,
Bruce Turner; Front row L-R: Frank Parr, Robin Rathborne, Wally Fawkes, Ray Smith

Jack Hobbs who was travelling with the team as a journalist and a few days later met him at a garden party and beat him at tennis, although Turner admitted, "I don't think he was trying very hard." As a teenager, Turner attended Dulwich College in South London, a contemporary of future Essex and England Test player Trevor Bailey, and lived in Blackheath. Here he played cricket on the heath and visited Lords and the Oval to see local heroes Patsy Hendren and Alf Gover. It was at this time he became interested in jazz, through his elder brother, Tren, who introduced him to the music of Duke Ellington, Fletcher Henderson and Frankie Trumbauer, starting a career which saw Turner playing clarinet and alto with the bands of Humphrey Lyttelton, Acker Bilk and Freddy Randall, as well as leading his own Jump Band. He also accompanied such illustrious Americans as Buck Clayton, Ben Webster, Bill Coleman, Wild Bill Davison, Don Byas, Big Bill Broonzy, Henry Red Allen, Eddie Condon and Sidney Bechet .

A mainstreamer, despite taking lessons from Lee Konitz and hearing Charlie Parker in New York when he was working the cross-Atlantic ships, Turner modelled his alto playing on Charlie Holmes, Benny Carter and Johnny Hodges. Ironic then, when playing at Birmingham Town Hall with the Humphrey Lyttelton Band in 1953,

Frank Parr leads Ravers off field, 1961; L-R Ray Smith, Cliff Wren, umpire Denis Povey, Bob Dawbarn (far rear), Wally Fawkes, Robin Rathborne, Glyn Morgan, Jim Godbolt and umpire Harry Hines

that some ardent traditionalists unfurled a banner which read "GO HOME DIRTY BOPPER," aimed at Turner's presence.

Jazz writer and critic Max Jones played for the team early in its history "He was a fine batsman," recalled Jim Godbolt, "a good catcher of the ball and, of course, had a word or two before, during and after the game. When his wicket fell, the immediate fielders would be the first to receive a detailed analysis of what went wrong, and we would see him continuing on his way back, becoming more and more audible as he

Wally Fawkes, Ray Smith, Malcolm Hoskinson, late 50s

Pete Appleby, Gerry Wright, Naomi Crowder, Ray Smith, Bob Dawbarn, late 50s

Wally Fawkes playing tenor, with Jeremy French tbne, Dave Wilkins tpt, Ray Smith d, Geoff Kemp b and Colin Purbrook p.c1960/1

approached the pavilion, where the scenario was re-run." He was known to 'like a chat', as Billie Holiday once told Max's wife, Betty: "Max sure does love me, but couldn't you stop him talking me to death." Writer Brian Case, a colleague at *Melody Maker* and close friend (and referred to by Max as 'Junior Beret'), described this loquaciousness as a "verbal slip stream."

Max was a great character on the British jazz scene and was respected throughout the jazz world, mixing with the cream of its history, including Billie Holiday, Coleman Hawkins, Lester Young and Eddie Condon. On their first meeting, Condon accepted a swig from Max's whisky flask and looking at Max's hairless, bereted head quipped, "Don't give me the name of your hairdresser, just your distiller." Max recalled introducing himself to Charlie Parker at the 1949 Paris Jazz Festival – "Parker said "I know who you are," and he gave me a pretty firm look. You felt that what he knew of you was strictly to your disadvantage."

Ben Webster and Bill Coleman recorded *For Max* on their 1972 Black Lion album *Swingin' In London* and Buck Clayton's *One For Buck* (Columbia, 1961) included *Mr.Melody Maker*, dedicated to his friend. When Max retired, Tony Bennett turned up at his retirement party, Bob Dylan (who in his younger, unknown days had stayed with Max, at Woody Guthrie's request) sent a telegram. When he died, the *Telegraph* included a photo of him armed with a wind-up gramophone, a tin of steel needles and a 78rpm record, made in 1930, of Jimmie Rodgers singing *Blue Yodel No.9*, asking Louis Armstrong if he was the trumpet player in such unlikely company. An astonished Armstrong verified that he was and Max, not lost for hyperbole, reported it in his *Melody Maker* column, *Collector's Corner*. The headline read, "CORNER SCOOPS THE WORLD ON 1930 ARMSTRONG DISC."

Jim Godbolt first met Max in 1941 at the No.1 Rhythm Club and visited the famous Jig's Club in Soho with him, hearing Cyril Blake's band. Their friendship continued until Max's death in August 1993. A month before, Godbolt had interviewed the American drummer Roy Haynes for *Jazz at Ronnie Scott's* magazine: "the one person he enquired after was Max, who, I am happy to report was voluble to the end."

Drummer and manager of Collets Jazz Shop (later Ray's), Ray Smith, was a long-serving member of the team. As a 'modernist' amongst many traddies and mainstream jazzers, Ray took some flak, especially on his debut when the caustic Mick Mulligan started singing *I Ain't Got No Body* on seeing Ray's unathletic, skeletal body in the changing room. But Ray was a spin bowler of great skill, taking over 1,000 wickets for the team and such was his reputation that a rival club invited him on tour. In one match, Ray took all nine wickets to fall when the last batsman came in. It was the last ball of his over and he decided to improvise – change his style by bowling absolutely straight, simply varying the pace and flight. This had the desired effect as the final batsman missed the ball which hit his pad directly in front of the stumps. A clear leg before wicket and all ten wickets for Ray. To his astonishment the umpire judged it not out. The bowler at the other end then took the tenth wicket and Ray missed out. In the club house after the match, over a drink, Ray questioned the decision and the umpire agreed it was plumb lbw, but added that as the batsman in question was chairman of the club, he had no intention of giving him out first ball. Enough said!

Later in the early 80s, this ability and prowess led to Ray being asked to advise young spin bowlers at the nets at Lords, where he could be seen watching matches with drummer Charlie Watts, another ardent follower of the game, or with his close friend, improvising musician Paul Shearsmith. In his earlier drumming days, Ray was in Wally Fawkes' band that also had Dave Wilkins on trumpet, so one can imagine the cricketing conversation in the band room. It was around this time that Ray got to know Charlie Watts. According to Ray, at one point Watts, then playing in a support band, borrowed Ray's drumkit, but unfortunately put a hole in one of the drumheads. He gave Ray a few pounds to get it mended which never happened. For many years the kit remained in the basement at Collet's Jazz Shop, then at Ray's, complete with the homemade patch Ray used as a repair. The money, Ray said, simply used to buy a drink or two.

Ravers 1961: Back: Cliff Wren, Denis Povey, John Robinson, Jim Godbolt, Mick Mulligan, Glyn Morgan, Bob Dawbarn. Seated: David Miller, Wally Fawkes, Frank Parr, Robin Rathborne, Ray Smith

Although renowned as a member of the Rolling Stones, Watts started out playing in blues and jazz bands and retained his enthusiasm for jazz, later reflected in his stellar Big Band that played at Ronnie Scott's and in New York in the mid 1980s. From early days on his first instrument, the banjo, and listening to the Johnny Dodds Trio, his uncle's jazz 78s, Armstrong, Ellington and Earl Bostic, he moved on to more modern tastes – Gerry Mulligan, Chico Hamilton, Thelonious Monk and in particular Charlie Parker. In the early 1960s he wrote and illustrated a children's book *Ode To a Highflying Bird* about the saxophonist. A lifelong follower of cricket, which he played at Tylers Croft Secondary Modern School as a boy, he still regularly goes to matches, often with Mick Jagger. In 2014, after a sell-out concert in Adelaide, Don Bradman's son, John, took them on a tour of the Bradman Museum at the Adelaide Oval. Posing with the ICC World Cup Trophy, Jagger joked that he was as close to the trophy as any Englishman was going to get.

Former agent (of the Dankworth Seven), manager (of George Webb's Dixielanders and the Mick Mulligan Band), writer of *Jazz in Britain* 1919-1950, amongst others, and editor of *Jazz Illustrated* and *Jazz at Ronnie Scott's* magazines,

Jim Godbolt, wrote in his final memoirs *All This & Slowly Deteriorating Fast* (2013) about the pleasure in achieving his highest score for the Ravers. This was 45, including seven fours and one six, against Harrods in 1967.

"I don't recall any one of the seven fours, but I do have a vivid memory of the six, against some fast bowling. The production of a six – the lifting of the bat, the impact of bat and ball and the following through – is an operation encompassing mere seconds and generally precluding forethought. Adding six to the team score, and receiving the other batsman's compliments, was a priceless feeling, but it was over in seconds. I didn't know how near I was to the coveted 50 and Ray Smith, number eleven and batting last, walked down the pitch to warn me that a fourth stroke at this stage would see me and him back in the pavilion, our innings finished. Alas, I didn't pay heed to his warning and as I attempted to repeat the magic stroke I heard the fatal click behind me that told me I had been bowled out." Later, captain Frank Parr commented "If you can do it once, you can do it again," but it never occurred.

Godbolt got interested in cricket relatively late in life, in 1956, at the age of 32, and described his first game for the Ravers. The captain, Lyn Dutton, had set the field and he was directed to the deep in an unspecified position – "my feeling was that the further away the better was Dutton's thinking." An opposing batsman hit the ball high and Godbolt was aware it was coming in his direction. "I was standing in its path, immobile, my legs rooted to the ground, gaping at this ball coming towards me. It was only when it was a within a yard or so of my head that I was activated. At the very last minute I thrust up my right hand, opened my palm and the ball miraculously stuck." There was a cry of disbelief and congratulations from Frank Holder, and Godbolt felt pleased with himself, but more was to come. Later in the game a ball was again hit high, some distance away from him, so he ran blindly in the general direction and "lo and behold, the two hands I put up in the air caught this beast. A roar went up." This started his life as an enthusiastic member of the team, an ever-present over the next 20 years.

Ron Gould, writer and one-time manager of Dobells Blues and Folk Shop in Rathbone Place, London, also played for the Ravers. His cricket interest began when playing at school for Woolverstone Hall (an LCC grammar school) and subsequently for Old Woolverstonians, and he was a regular on the Soho folk/skiffle scene at the time, recalling heady days at The Skiffle Cellar, 49 Greek Street, which became the famous Les Cousins. When John Jack took over the Cellar on Friday and Saturday nights in 1957, he put on Bruce Turner's Jump Band, who he was then managing. Ron was a member of The Red Nerk Four skiffle group, which played there every other Friday night.

"There was one big night I remember, Jazz Against Apartheid, an all-nighter to raise money for Anti-Apartheid. It was a big night with Bruce, Humphrey Lyttelton and a special guest. We put together a band with me on bass, Diz Disley on guitar, Bruce and John Dankworth on altos, Lennie Hastings drums and Brian Lemon piano. Cleo Laine sang three songs. It was just about the highlight of my musical career."

He briefly played for the Ravers in 1964: "I remember the Mahoney brothers, Louis, but I do not remember the other one's name. They were both all-rounders and particularly fast bowlers. It was said that they played for The Gambia, but I have no confirmation of that."

The Ravers' club records from that time mention Louis by first name, but only have 'S.Mahoney' for the other – nevertheless, he seems to have been a good player. From all accounts this was Bola Mahoney, who was also known as 'Sam'. According to former Gambian cricketer and football player, George Gomez, he was an all-rounder and an exciting batsman, and one innings stood out for him. It was when The Gambia was playing against Sierra Leone and Mahoney had moved quickly to 90 when the tension kicked in as he approached a century. He slowly moved on to 98, then decided to attack, connecting with the ball but instead of the six the crowd were expecting it went to extra cover and was caught. "One could feel the disappoint-ment in the crowd and Bola slowing walked with tears in his eyes." (Gomez, *Sports and Culture in Colonial Gambia,* in *The Point*, July 7, 2017)

Born in the Gambia, West Africa in 1938, Louis Mahoney came to the UK in 1957 to study medicine but abandoned it to train at the (now Royal) Central School of Speech and Drama. It was during these early years in London that he regularly visited the 100 Club and other places, often with trumpeter Pat Halcox and his wife Shirley. Halcox had occasionally played cricket for the Ravers in the 50s, so it's highly likely that he introduced Mahoney to the team. Mahoney's musical interest also stretched to the blues and he was later to tell writer Val Wilmer of his visits to the Marquee Club, "When Muddy Waters was there" (so possibly 1958) and met Jack Bruce, Ginger Baker and Mick Jagger. He was also a friend of jazz promoter, driving force behind the National Jazz Federation and Marquee owner Harold Pendleton, and his wife, Barbara.

Mahoney worked in rep before joining the RSC in 1967, becoming one of the first black actors to appear with the company, and was seen in minor roles alongside Ian Richardson's Coriolanus, Ian Holm's Romeo and Estelle Kohler's Juliet. He also be-came the first Afro-Asian actor to be elected to Equity's council, in 1972, sitting on their Afro-Asian committee, and in 1976 launched the Black Theatre Workshop, with fellow actor Taiwo Ajai-Lycett and the writer Mike Phillips, to provide a plat-form for African writers and performers. Throughout his activism, Mahoney main-tained a steady acting career in theatre, on television and in films. His final stage ap-pearance was in Alan Bennett's *Allelujah!* at London's Bridge Theatre in 2018. He died in June 2020.

Certainly the Mahoneys made their mark in the period they played for the Ravers, in particular 'Sam'. In the pre-season warm-up game between the Ravers' Gentlemen and Players, on 2 May 1965, he scored 92 and took 5 wickets, an indica-tion of what was to come during that season, in which his highest score appears to have been 84 not out against Kensington Argyll, and his batting average was a com-mendably consistent 29.87. However, generally it was his bowling that impressed. 1963 saw returns of 6 wickets for 70 against Vic Lewis' XI and 7 for 53 against Valley End, in a season in which he took 38 wickets at 14.73. The following year he took 51 wickets at 14.72, including 5 for 19 against Ashtead Cross Arrows and 6 for 26

Frank Parr, Ray Smith and the author watch the cricket, Ravers CC reunion match 2004

against Pan American. It was that year, 1964, that one 'E.Mahoney', possibly a cousin, also had a few outings for the team.

Over the years there were other notable bowling performances: drummer Terry Seymour taking 7 wickets for 67 runs in 1961 against The Eclectics; trombonist Campbell Burnap's 7-32 in his first season, 1971, against Balcombe; fast bowler Robin May's impressive figures of 8 overs, 5 maidens, 5 wickets for 9 runs against Penn & Tylers Green in 1972; Wally Fawkes' 5-42 against Vic Lewis Xl in 1961; Ray Smith's 5 for 9 runs against Hestair in 1964 and his 7-18 against Elstree in 1971, a season in which he took 91 wickets at an average of 12.92. These were performances of players who took their cricket seriously, at least on the field of play. The later performances in the club house less so.

"One of the things about The Ravers was that we were all very serious about cricket and wanted good games," recalled Ron Gould, "some of the teams and places we played were expecting a 'show biz' team hoping that Acker (Bilk) or Kenny Ball would be playing."

An indication of the seriousness in which they held their games was the copious record-keeping, seasonal averages and statistics. Some years it even included short reports of games. Against BroomWade (a factory team from High Wycombe) at Paddington on 21 June 1970 the report shows that BroomWade made 191 for 5 declared. In response, the Ravers scored 192 for 3, winning by 7 wickets. There follows: "(Andy) Wheeler came in when Lovell was run out – no accident – with the score at 121 for 3, and he and (Malcolm) Hoskinson put on 71 in 22 minutes. This stand produced the fastest run-rate ever recorded by the Ravers even though some time was spent looking for a lost ball. A suspicious incident this. Three or four fielders failed to find the ball until one of the batsmen sprinted to the boundary when it was miraculously produced. The winning run was scored off the penultimate ball of the last over of the day. 71 was scored off 31 balls, only one of which failed to score a run. On the way back to the pavilion, the shorter of the two somewhat portly batsmen had to stop twice to rest."

Over the years, many involved felt the character of the side had changed, that the 'jazz' aspect had largely been lost, despite the presence of some involved in the music. However, 2004 saw the fiftieth anniversary of the Ravers, and a reunion match was played at Dulwich College. Many of the old players had died, others couldn't make it, but among those present were Frank Parr, pianist George Webb, bassist Jim Bray, drummers Richie Bryant and Terry Seymour, Nick Jones (son of Max), Campbell Burnap, Jeff Horton, Martin Ash, and many more. The late Robin Rathborne, who was possibly the team's most prolific batsman from the 1950s to the 70s, was represented by his cricket-playing sons. Of the cricket that was played, Jim Godbolt wrote of David and Andrew Rathborne: "the latter catching the former off sixty-five year old Burnap's rusty bowling. A tad of sibling rivalry here! Drummer Richie Bryant batted neatly and the 100 Club's Jeff Horton was impressively athletic. Many players left limping happily and then upheld the Ravers' perennial reputation as enthusiastic patrons of the bar." (*Jazz at Ronnie Scotts* magazine, October 2004)

7

Bebop and Beyond

For many years, pianist George Shearing and his wife relocated from their New York home to Stow-on-the-Wold in the Cotswolds for a few months each summer. Here Shearing would listen to *Test Match Special* on BBC Radio and when cricket commentator Brian Johnston heard of this, he invited Shearing to the 1990 New Zealand Test match at Lords and interviewed him for *View from the Boundary*. Johnston had met Shearing once before, at Fischer's Restaurant in London in 1946, when Shearing was with the Frank Weir Band and Johnston was broadcasting *Saturday Night Out*.

Shearing described his life in the Linden Lodge School for the Blind, Wandsworth, where he attended between the ages of 12 and 16 and where he played cricket, at first with a large balloon-type ball with a bell in it (he was later to joke "you needed the bell for the shortsighted"), underarm bowling and a wicket made of wooden blocks and plywood. "As a kid" (in Battersea) he recalled, "I used to go out in the street and play cricket with sighted people," with him holding the bat helped by one of the local boys. "Sometimes I hit the ball and sometimes it hit me." When imagining the play, Shearing admitted to having only vision of light and dark, but sitting in the commentary box "it's an interesting aspect of controlled acoustics and wonderful daylight." He would have to imagine the proceedings: "Two things that a born-blind man would have difficulty with are colour and perspective," but his education and instruction had given him the information to deal with spatial issues. During the interview he recalled listening to pioneering BBC commentator Howard Marshall on the radio throughout the thirties, including the description of Len Hutton's famous innings of 364 for England against Australia at the Oval in 1938.

A chance encounter happened for sports writer David Foot : "I found myself talking to a blind man for whom a companion was giving a running commentary. 'How I love cricket and desperately wish I could see the play.' He was George Shearing, the great jazz pianist who liked to be taken to a Gloucestershire match during summer visits to this country" (*Guardian* 2009). Foot, an insightful and often reflective writer, described this as one of his saddest moments in cricket.

After his knighthood ceremony in 2007, Shearing hosted a luncheon for close friends including fellow cricket enthusiasts Michael Parkinson and John Dankworth.

In his book *Jazz in Revolution* (1998), John Dankworth wrote that amongst his contemporaries at school was Doug Insole, later of Essex and England and author of *Cricket Notes* for *Jazz Express*, the Pizza Express in-house magazine. Dankworth described his Dankworth Seven band as more of a social unit, as they spent so much leisure time together. They were all cricket fans, and frequently visited Lords to watch Middlesex, especially when Denis Compton and Bill Edrich were batting. On one occasion they went to watch England play the West Indies, which included the famous 'three Ws': Weekes, Worrell and Walcott. When arriving at Lords, and seeing the 'House Full' notice, bassist Joe Mudele singled out a block of flats flanking the ground, marched the rest of the band up several flights of stairs and knocked on a random door, saying "Sorry to bother you, but we've come to see the cricket and the ground is full. Could we watch from your window?"

"I marvelled with some embarrassment at Joe's impudence" recalled Dankworth. "We all trooped in to a sea of welcoming faces, the crucial windows were cleared and equipped with chairs and we spent the whole of that day – and the next – enjoying a grandstand view of the action."

A contemporary of Dankworth was the saxophonist, writer and broadcaster Benny Green, who played saxophone in the bands of Ralph Sharon (1952), Ronnie Scott (1952), Stan Kenton (1956), Dizzy Reece (1957) and in Lord Rockingham's Xl (1958). He wrote extensively about cricket, editing the *Wisden Anthologies*, summaries of the famous cricket annual, and *The Wisden Book of Obituaries* (1986), and writing *A History of Cricket* (1988), *Benny Green's Cricket Archive* (1985) and others. He became a successful broadcaster, chairing BBC's *Jazz Score* and wrote for *Punch*, *The Spectator* and other periodicals.

Another musician to play with Dankworth was Guyanese singer and percussionist Frank Holder, a keen cricketer who played for Vic Lewis' Celebrity teams and for the Ravers C.C. Born in Georgetown, Guyana in 1925, Holder first heard jazz on late night broadcasts from the USA. He served in the RAF before embarking on a career in music, joining the band of Leslie 'Jiver' Hutchinson in 1946. Following gigs with trumpeter Kenny Baker, he came to the attention of John Dankworth, joining his Seven in 1950. He made several recordings for Decca, Parlophone and London Records and played with a great many of the established names in British jazz – Ronnie Scott, Tubby Hayes, Don Rendell, Peter King, Harry Beckett, Shake Keane, Coleridge Goode, Ronnie Ross, Joe Harriott, and many more. He even branched out into variety and cabaret performances. In more recent years he played with Mornington Lockett, Dave O'Higgins and on Steve Waterman's 2006 album *Our Delight: A Jazz Odyssey* he contributed a Nat King Cole-inspired *If You Could See Me Now*. In 2011, Holder performed at the gala jazz event *A Tribute to John Dankworth and the Big Band* at the Queen Elizabeth Hall and continued to work into his nineties.

A keen sportsman, as a young man he was a boxer and sprinter, and during his musical career he played in numerous cricket teams, many for charity events with cricket celebrities including West Indians Gary Sobers and Wes Hall.

This West Indian connection has understandably been present, given the historical links and the huge following cricket has in the Caribbean. When writing about Alf Lindsay's club, Birdland, in South London's Stockwell Park Crescent, in the magazine *Jazzwise* (March 2013), Val Wilmer mentioned the visitors that would on occasion drop by. A "vibrant jazz club that flourished for nearly three years at the turn of the 1960s... the club was a rarity among black-operated venues in being devoted to jazz, with Lindsay partially reflected in his name. He called himself 'Emanuel Bird', with a plaque on his piano telling aspiring jamsters: 'Ornithologist:

if you don't like Bird, you don't play here.'" The reference to Charlie Parker obvious for those in the know. Regulars included trumpeter Eddie 'Tan Tan' Thornton and saxophonists Rudy Jones, Roy Burrell and Mikey Elliott. As a student in London, Nigerian and future Afrobeat pioneer Fela Kuti dropped in, and there were reports that Count Basie trumpeter Thad Jones had also done so. "Calypsonian Young Kitch (the Pretender) hung out after Mayfair gigs... plus a West Indies team cricketer, and distinguished film actor James Mason." On further investigation, the cricketer turned out to be fast bowler Roy Gilchrist.

A controversial figure, Gilchrist was a hostile and often volatile bowler, whose career in top-class cricket was sadly brief, terminated in a startling manner when he was sent home from the West Indies tour of India in 1959 for disciplinary reasons. Gilchrist was a small man, but generated tremendous pace. He made a considerable impression in the tour of England in 1957, despite incurring an injury part-way through the tour, taking ten wickets in four Tests. On the tour of India in 1959, he formed an intimidating opening partnership with Wes Hall. His finest performance was in the Third Test where he took 3 wickets for 18 runs followed by 6 for 55 as part of a massive West Indies win (an innings and 336 runs). However, in a subsequent match, Gilchrist let fly a sequence of very fast bouncers, interspersed with a beamer, which combined with off-field altercations with captain Gerry Alexander, resulted in him being sent home.

Michael Manley, in his *History of West Indies Cricket*, called Gilchrist's loss a tragedy, saying however that "Gilchrist was difficult, insufferably so at times. He was also potentially, a very great bowler". Gilchrist took 57 wickets in 13 Tests at an average of 26.68.

In his autobiography, *Hit Me For Six* (1963), he attempted to put over a different side of his character to that of his reputation as a "wild boy": "I like fine clothes that are dark and snappy, with white shirts, black shoes, dark ties and clean hankies. Perry Como, Nat King Cole, progressive jazz and a good night out... the odd whisky never did me any harm either." He didn't elaborate on what he meant by "progressive jazz" but maybe he'd been listening to *It's All in the Game* from Nat Cole's album *Love Is the Thing* (1957): "Many a tear has to fall, but it's all in the game..."

Following the India tour, Gilchrist moved to England and played successfully in the Lancashire League, then in 1962-3, somewhat ironically given his treatment of the Indian batsmen, for Hyderabad, as one of four West Indians invited to take part in domestic Indian cricket to improve their players' batting technique against fast bowling. According to Hyderabad batsman M.L. Jaisimha, in his biography *My Way* (2005) written by Joseph Anthony and Jayanthi Jaisimha (MLJ's wife): "Not surprisingly, parents of Bengal players had their sons insured for the match against Hyderabad. Many of them wore sponge pads to protect their chest and thighs."

Gilchrist lived in England before moving back to Jamaica in 1985, where he died in 2001.

There are many other examples of jazz musicians being involved with the sport. When Jim Laker famously took 19 wickets in the Test against Australia at Old Trafford in 1956 (first innings figures: 51.2 overs, 23 maidens, 10 wickets for 53 runs; match figures 68 overs, 27 maidens, 19 wickets for 90 runs) Tubby Hayes dedicated a number, *Laker's Day*, in recognition of the performance. Recorded as *Live at the Flamingo*, despite being at the Railway Arms, West Hampstead, the band shouts "Howzat!" at the end of the number. The personnel was Ronnie Scott and Tubby Hayes (tenor saxes), Harry Klein (baritone sax), Terry Shannon (piano), Lennie Bush (bass) and Tony Crombie (drums). Tony Hall, who co-produced and introduced the session, later wrote in his column *Hall Hears* in the *Record Mirror*, August 1957, that "many modernists are ardent cricket enthusiasts" and referred to Hayes spending most of his free time at the Oval cricket ground. Also mentioned was a Tubby Hayes XI which played against a team organised by drummer Terry Seymour on Clapham Common. Participants included Allan Ganley, Phil Bates, Joe Temperley, Phil Seamen and Joe Harriott. The game was helped somewhat, Hall suggested, by the proximity of the pitch to a pub. Spike Wells who played with Tubby (Brian) Hayes in the late 60s/early 70s and himself a member of the MCC and Sussex County Cricket Club:

> I knew Tubby liked cricket – we watched a programme about Gary Sobers together and, when he died, Liz (Grunlund) gave me a dog-eared copy of *Testing Time for England* signed, by its author, 'To Brian. Best wishes Denis Compton'.

For many years The Outswingers, a band formed by saxophonist Johnny Barnes and including over the years American tenor player Spike Robinson (a member at Essex C.C.C.) and trombonists Campbell Burnap and Roy Williams, have regularly entertained the crowd at Lords during Test matches. A band performing at cricket matches was nothing new. It has happened regularly at the Scarborough Cricket Festival and as far back as 1862, when the All England XI played Doncaster, the crowd were entertained by the 1st West York Yeomanry Cavalry Band. However, it tended to be a brass or military band on these occasions.

The Outswingers have played at several benefits for professional cricketers and one included bass saxophonist Harry Gold who asked Johnny Barnes to sponsor him as a member of the exclusive MCC. Barnes told him that there was an eighteen year wait to be a member, to which Gold replied, "That's OK, I can wait." He was seventy-five at the time. Had he persisted with his application, he could have had two years membership, as Gold died at the age of ninety-five.

Born in Belper, Derbyshire, in 1939, Campbell Burnap listened to Bunk Johnson and George Lewis as a teenager with friend, clarinettist Chris Blount. He emigrated to New Zealand in 1959 and started playing trombone regularly there and in Australia before returning, via the USA, to Britain, where he joined the bands of Terry Lightfoot, then Monty Sunshine. After another period in Australia, he settled back in Britain, playing with Alan Elsdon's Dixieland band, Acker Bilk and others. His style was influenced by Jack Teagarden and Vic Dickenson, one of whose trombones Burnap bought.

Given the precarious nature of the jazz business, he decided as financial back up to get a teaching qualification, so enrolled at Furzedown College of Education in Tooting, South London, but instead of sitting his final exams he went to a cricket

Spike Wells and Tubby Hayes, *courtesy Spike Wells*

Tubby Hayes behind the bar at Ronnie Scott's, 1964. Left to right:
Freddy Logan, Allan Ganley, Tubby Hayes, Jimmy Deuchar, Terry Shannon,
courtesy Bruce Fleming

match at Lords, after which he supported his income as a film extra. His reputation as a fine trombonist, however, gave him plenty of work and he was called on to support visiting musicians, such as Wild Bill Davison and Ruby Braff. He also worked for the BBC, Jazz FM, local radio and even as a cricket commentator for British Telecom's *Cricketcall* during the 1990 County Championship.

He had always been interested in cricket and played regularly for the Ravers Cricket Club and, as a member of Derbyshire County Cricket Club for 20 years, had developed a friendship with the former Derbyshire and England player Geoff Miller. As a member of the Outswingers, he regularly entertained the crowds at the intervals at Lords, performing for the last time when England played New Zealand in May 2008, only a few weeks before his death. Following his funeral, a memorial celebration was held in the Long Room at Lords, after which his ashes were sprinkled, appropriately, in the Harris Gardens, where the Outswingers would play at all the Test matches.

Originally from Manchester, Roy Williams moved to London in his early 20s and became a regular member of Alex Welsh's band, along with Johnny Barnes. He then spent a number of years with Humphrey Lyttelton and has consistently been an award-winning trombonist since, as well as a sideman for visiting jazz players, such as Ruby Braff, Wild Bill Davison, Bud Freeman, Buddy Tate, Doc Cheatham, Bob Wilber and many others. He played with Burnap in the trombone ensemble, Five-a-Slide.

Fellow Mancunian Johnny Barnes moved to London in the mid-50s, and like Williams, worked with the bands of Welsh, Lyttelton and many others. He would often introduce numbers by the Outswingers altering the title with reference to cricket, so *Willow Weep For Me* would become *Willow Sweep For Me*; *You Go To My Head* as *You Throw To My Head*; and *Red Sails In The Sunset* as *Red Bails In The Sunset*. He has played at the Nice Jazz Festival with the Jazz Journal All-Stars and co-led groups with Alan Barnes, with fellow cricket follower, Bruce Turner, and was part of Tenor Madness with Spike Robinson and Bobby Wellins.

Venkatraman Ramnarayan, right arm off-spinner for Hydrabad in the 1970s, a regular columnist for *Cricinfo*, and editor of *Sruti*, a monthly performing arts magazine, once recalled "The late Test batsman ML Jaisimha, under whose captaincy I played for Hyderabad in the Ranji Trophy, had an impressive voice with which he belted out popular songs. He brought the roof down at a restaurant at Bangkok back in 1978 when the resident band handed him the microphone and he gave a few lusty samples of his Frank Sinatra repertoire and Louis Armstrong's *When the Saints Go Marching In*."

There is the story about Jaisimha, that on his way to the West Indies test tour in 1962, he stopped in New York to hang out with his brother Pratap Simha and a friend called Dicky. They commenced a pub crawl, ending up at a jazz bar where Ella Fitzgerald was performing but got upset when they couldn't meet her backstage after the show. Pratap caused a fuss and was thrown out, not before threatening "I know the senator!" Ella came out to see what the commotion was about. Jaisimha and Dicky explained to her that they had travelled all the way from India just to meet her, and, quite possibly due to Jaisimha's famous charm, she not only gave him an autographed photograph, inscribed *'With love to Jai'*, but a huge hug too, at which point Dicky apparently burst into tears; such is the power alcohol has on the emotions.

Kuldip Singh wrote in Jaisimha's obituary (*Independent*, September 9, 1999) that he was a superb player of spin with nimble footwork and unorthodox style which was a delight to watch, whilst Australian cricketer and commentator Jack Fingleton described him as a debonair and elegant batsman, with correct upright stance, free and flawless backswing and exemplary footwork. Jaisimha's teammate Abbas Ali Baig said that his audacious batting could light up a stadium. He was also remembered for his droll sense of humour and ability to regale people for hours with hilarious, irreverent anecdotes.

On the website *Madhuradhwani – music & beyond,* Ramnarayan also mentioned American writer Mike Marqusee, who wrote "I would have loved to hear John Coltrane explore the Pancharatna kritis." (Hindu songs in Carnatic classical music). Marqusee was known for his writings on politics, music and cricket, which he started watching whilst a student at Sussex University. Moving from New York to Britain in 1971, he took an active interest in politics, editing *Labour Left Briefing*, writing for *Left Unity* and the *Guardian*, and becoming an executive member of the *Stop the War Coalition* and the *Socialist Alliance.*

In his article *Why Cricket?* (2014) Marqusee put forward the idea of most sports being wonderfully pointless, having their own means and ends, which is central to their appeal. "Whatever social function is assigned to them, they exceed that function, impose their own demands and disciplines, and beguile the spectator in their own manner... (they) offer a living mixture of the abstract and concrete, the impersonal and the personal, fixed laws and ceaseless spontaneity." Certainly there can be parallels drawn here with jazz, and his ideas are taken further in the involvement of the spectator, who can bestow all manner of significance on it. "We are not just 'consumers' of cricket. Watching is not a passive process; it engages a range of faculties – imagination, interpretation, memory." In this respect, it corresponds with that of the listener, whose perception may be highly personal, differ from others, and make reference to tunes, songs and styles recalled from the past. This interpretation of what is heard may then be entirely subjective or objective.

There are numerous other links between cricket and jazz and very often clubhouses are used as jazz venues. Some of my earliest recollections of both were at Didsbury cricket ground, where my father went to hear pianist Ken Frith play jazz and where he took me to a Brian Statham benefit match on the rest day of the 1961 Old Trafford test. The whole of the Australian team turned up for it – a schoolboy's dream come true. As I recall, Basil D'Oliviera, then with Lancashire League team Middleton, played for the All Star XI against the local Didsbury Cricket Club, with BBC commentator Brian Johnston keeping wicket.

8

The Outfield

David Toop, in his book *Into The Maelstrom: Music, Improvisation and the Dream of Freedom* (2016), makes the useful distinction between free improvisation and free jazz, which retains ties to theme and variation. Free improvisation affects how a piece of music develops, and as in life, the individual has to learn to cope and deal with random events, the influence and contributions of others (negative or otherwise), success, failure, chaos, disaster and accident. There might be a degree of planning and structure, but for an improviser like Toop, there is the risk that this can be insidious and have too much of a controlling effect. This is where it departs from improvisation within jazz, which has a framework and 'rules' which have to adhered to, to a certain extent. But in both, the improvisation allows the individual to express character, respond to other musicians and to the audience, and to explore possibilities using their own frame of references, opening up a wider field of potentialities. It doesn't necessarily exclude the pre-written framework that makes it possible. Toop also refers to an interview that jazz trumpeter Don Ellis (known for his forays into improvisation and experimentation) had with Richard Williams for the *Melody Maker* in 1970 : "It's not a case of getting up and just blowing what you want... for me it has to make musical sense and have an interesting framework." This however is in contrast to the free improviser who may see the context of musical scores and even technique as counter-productive, even as baggage. There are parallels, as Ian Botham has been reported as saying, "Cricket is full of theorists who can ruin your game in no time."

But just as jazz solos are constructed within a framework, conforming to timing, standardised pitch and suchlike, so cricket is played according to rules, techniques and pre-learned skills. Not just the obvious ones of how to hold a bat/bowl, etc, but also the finer honed skills and nuances – marginal differences in stance, guard taken, shot selection. And it doesn't necessarily have to do with finesse: "He had no style and yet he was all style. He had three strokes for every ball." So wrote C.B. Fry about the Australian batsman Victor Trumper.

In bowling there are differences of arm or wrist action, finger position, fluctuations at the moment of delivery, all which changes the performance and potentially the outcome, not only of the individual's implementation but of the result of the game. In totally free improvisation it could be argued that the instrument need not be played in the accepted way – the saxophone bell used as a vocal sound box, the guitar as a percussive instrument – or non-standard objects utilised. Of course this is where it veers away from a cricket analogy. A logical extension might be the batsman picking up a stump to hit the ball; the ball being bowled in a completely opposite direction; a run being taken not between stumps but towards the boundary rope. A potentially comical, anarchic scene – not one for the purists.

In Berlin, October 2011 a group of British musicians recorded a set of improvisations that were issued as *Just Not Cricket*, featuring Lol Coxhill, Trevor Watts, Steve Beresford, John Edwards, Gail Brand, Shabaka Hutchings, Phil Minton, Orphy Robinson and others. Performed over a number of days, they play solo and in a variety of ad-hoc ensembles. In organising the project, Antoine Prum wanted to see if there was a specifically British element in free improvisation, compared for example with the *Total Music Meetings* that had occurred in Germany. Describing the recordings, Colin Green wrote on the *Free Jazz Collective* website:

> This is improvisation in which things are taken apart and reassembled in new and fascinating ways... there are times when no voice predominates: everything is group texture... sometimes combinations break off to pursue their own agenda... not all the conversations are polite... there's a juxtaposition between order and unruliness... restlessness and spontaneity.

Explaining the title, Green's view is that as an expression meaning 'not the done thing' or 'unacceptable', it "might be typically British irony or simply a reference to a sport whose appeal is baffling to anyone outside Britain and her former colonies." Given that, it's a shame that instead of the musicians being assigned items of the construction industry as pieces of identification (harpist Rhodri Davies was given a fretsaw, bassist Dominic Lash a bag of cement and pianist Matthew Bourne a spirit level) they weren't allotted items of cricket paraphernalia – umpires' stones, a cricket glove, a light meter, a bail, a cricket box, etc.

The results are intriguing – both in terms of length and in some having greater success than others, though of course this is entirely subjective. For those of a certain inclination, the recordings are well worth hearing more than once, and with all good examples of improvisation, there are things that newly appear to the listener on each occasion.

This was one of Lol Coxhill's last recordings, before his death in July 2012 at the age of 79, a man who made a huge contribution to music both as improviser and jazz performer, and good company – a witty, erudite man and great raconteur. He had musical connections with several of those mentioned elsewhere in this book including Bruce Turner and Wally Fawkes.

There have been many examples of collaborations in which the improvisation has been indebted to jazz but not restricted by its framework. From the a cappella stylings of Coleman Hawkins and Sonny Rollins, through the duets of Lennie Tristano and Lee Konitz, Max Roach and Abdullah Ibrahim, to present day, there have always been ways of ways of exploring the music's possibilities whilst retaining its musical basis in jazz.

For our purposes, the way musicians play together, interacting and responding to each other, whether in free improvisation or in the more structured contexts of jazz composition and even Free Jazz, could be seen to have parallels in cricket. This could be duets or collective playing, similar or contrasting styles – Wardell Gray's light sound and speed with Dexter Gordon's full, voluminous tone; Miles Davis' lyrical, laid-back and carefully poised tightness and John Coltrane's assertive hard tone, bursting with urgency; Joe Venuti's forceful violin and Eddie Lang's perceptive, attentive chords and single note runs. These can correspond to partnerships and collaborations in cricket. Bowlers have often operated in tandem – the aggression and unpredictability of Fred Trueman and the relentless accuracy and subtlety of Brian Statham – when Frank Tyson partnered Statham, he put his success down to his partner's "relentless pursuit" that injected desperation into the batsmen: "it felt like having Menuhin playing second fiddle to my lead"; Michael Holding's speed and stealth with the consistency and deception of Malcolm Marshall; the guile, grace, flight and rhythm of the quartet of off-spinners Chandresekhar and Prasanna, leg break of Venkataraghavan and left arm spin of Bedi, that dominated spin bowling in the 1960s and 70s.

Batsmen have also shown contrasting styles in partnership. The elegance and classicism of David Gower and the force and belligerence of Ian Botham; the technique and assertive determination of Sachin Tendulkar and defensive solidity of Rahul Dravid; the fearless and destructive Viv Richards with anyone.

"The conjunction at the creases of C.B. Fry and K.S. Ranjitsinhji," wrote Neville Cardus (*Wisden*, 1957)

> was a sight and an appeal to the imagination not likely ever to be repeated; Fry, nineteenth-century rationalist, batting according to first principles with a sort of moral grandeur, observing patience and abstinence. At the other end of the wicket, 'Ranji' turned a cricket bat into a wand of conjuration.

The *Sydney Mail* reported on England's match at the Oval on August 22, 1934 and the complementary partnership of Australians Don Bradman and Bill Ponsford, an indication of how two players using their technique, their collaborative and individual skills, and their reading of the situation, responded to the game and shaped the outcome.

> The reaction of the two batsmen to short bumpers from Bowes and Clark was decidedly interesting. Ponsford has two ways of dealing with these. He either turns his head and allows them to hit him in the middle of the back or backs away and cuts the ball down the gully. Bradman's method is more spectacular - and more artistic, as he moves into the line of flight and smashes the ball toward the leg boundary. From this combination of smash, hook, and pull Bradman scored ten fours in the region of square-leg, not to mention seven past mid-on, which were from balls pitched further up. Ponsford had only one four in the square-leg area, and that was off Verity... After

the interval both batsmen pelted the tiring bowlers, Ponsford to every part of the off-side boundary and Bradman to every point of the compass.

They had broken their own record for the highest partnership by putting on 451 runs. Bradman's contribution was 244 at nearly a run a minute; Ponsford going on to 266. When the stand had passed 300, English player Herbert Sutcliffe ran to collect the ball after another Bradman boundary, put his hands on the boundary rails and asked the crowd with a smile: "Anyone got any suggestions?"

In each partnership the players could be seen working towards a successful outcome, based on mutual performance and interaction, so changing the course, and result, of a game. The parallel can be seen in musical partnerships.

Perhaps the most curious link between improvised music and cricket is Canadian percussionist Chris Corsano's CD *The Young Cricketer* (2006). Corsano has regularly played with American jazz saxophonist Paul Flaherty, but also with Evan Parker and with bassist John Edwards. On *The Young Cricketer* he uses a collection of instruments, musical and otherwise: drums, cymbals, saxophone mouthpieces, tubes, pots and pans, balls on sticks and other things. Although when asked, Corsano said he has no real interest in cricket and the idea came about through a friend when he lived in Manchester, but although it has no apparent connection as such, the track titles would appear quite the opposite!

Track listing:
1. What do we mean by coaching?
2. How should you pick up the ball and throw it?
3. What do people mean when they say 'He played cricket'?
4. What do we get from cricket that we don't get from other games?
5. If you want to succeed at cricket what attitude should you adopt towards the game?
6. How may your parents and your employer help you in your cricket career?
7. What is the correct way to stop a ball?
8. How do you know that you have taken you eyes off the ball when you attempt to catch it?
9. Why are some cricket coaches better than others?
10. How will you learn more successfully from your coach than by just looking and listening?
11. What movement helps you when you are trying to run out a batsman?
12. Why should you watch the strikers bat?
13. How do you know where to throw the ball?
14. When should you throw the ball at top speed?
15. How should you throw it on other occasions?
16. Are you going to keep alive the spirit of cricket?

At one point... Corsano even duos with himself, hurling spittle through a piece of horn while simultaneously pounding out a blurry beat. But that's just the tip of this massive iceberg, which drips with so many ideas and so much head-grabbing sound I almost wonder if Chris should retire now – this would easily qualify as the life-highlight of most sound-generating mortals. (Marc Masters, *Noiseweek*)

Praise indeed, and perhaps bringing to mind the case of Spike Hughes giving up his bass after what he considered the impossibility of achieving anything higher, following his playing with American jazz greats. Difficult in relating to cricket, unless it had a parallel with a description of someone reaching the pinnacle of their career then retiring; if Maurice Allom had, after his Test debut hat-trick, or more modestly, but still personally momentous, Jim Godbolt's top scoring 45 for the Ravers. It might be an individual performance that is difficult to imagine being bettered, such as Brian Lara's epic world record score of 501 for Warwickshire against Durham in 1994. A plethora of examples spring to mind in jazz: Django Reinhardt's solo in *Blue Drag* (1935); John Coltrane's *The Wise One* (1964); Bill Coleman's solo on *I'm In The Mood For Love* (1936); Betty Roche singing *Take the A Train* on *Ellington Uptown* (1952); Paul Gonsalves' 27 choruses of *Diminuendo and Crescendo in Blue* at the 1956 Newport Jazz Festival. All highly personal, often subjective choices but showing the individual expressions as responses to the situations in which the musicians find themselves.

These different approaches to improvisation might be seen as mirroring those in cricket. In April 2013, *Guardian* sports columnist Barney Ronay compared West Indian Chris Gayle's high-speed hundred off 30 balls for the Royal Challengers Bangalore with Billy Godleman's painstaking half century off 244 balls for Derbyshire in the same month. He saw a clash of tempo, textures and interpretation parallel to the violent airing of differences between traditional jazz fans and modernists, followers of the Bebop of Charlie Parker, during the Beaulieu Jazz Festival of 1960, but optimistically saw it as the indication of a new golden age of cricket and the meeting of "the be-bop fecundity of the new world and the enduring trad of the old."

Appendix – something for the statisticians

Courtesy Robert Lamb

Frank Parr: First-Class Cricket Career

Year	Opponents	Innings	Batting score	Dismissals
1951	Cambridge Uni	1st	b Warr 1	May c Parr b Berry 53
	Surrey	1st	c McIntyre b Surridge 0	Laker c Parr b Statham 7
		2nd	Not out 10	
1952	Hampshire	1st	b Cannings 4	Hill c Parr b Statham 0
		2nd	b Cannings 2	Rogers st Parr b Berry 17
				Shackleton st Parr b Berry 0
	Kent	1st	c Murray Wood b Page 13	Cowdrey st Parr b Wharton 23
				Wright c Parr b Tattershall 15
		2nd		Edrich c Parr b Lomax 61
	Middlesex	1st	Not out 26	Brown c Parr b Statham 9
				Compton c Parr b Statham 2
				Sharp c Parr b Hilton 14
	Northants	1st	lbw b Tribe 10	Livingston c Parr b Smith 2
	Somerset		Did not bat	
	Surrey	1st	Did not bat	Parker c Parr b Lomax 57
				Whittaker c Parr b Lomax 15
				McMahon c Parr b Statham 0
		2nd		Constable c Parr b Statham 11
				Whittaker c Parr B Lomax 4
	Sussex	1st	b Marlar 42	Langridge c Parr b Ikin 23
	Worcs	1st	st Yarnold b Jenkins 4	Yarnold st Parr b Berry 0
	Leics	1st	Not out 18	Lester c Parr b Wharton 25
				Jackson c Parr b Wharton 32
		2nd	c Spencer b Walsh 12	Smithson c Parr b Wharton 1
	Yorkshire	1st	b Trueman 5	Burgin c Parr b Berry 4
		2nd	Not out 9	Lowson c Parr b Statham 9
				Yardley c Parr b Lomax 10
	Sussex	1st	c Doggart b Oakman 0	Marlar c Parr b Wharton 1
				Webb c Parr b Statham 0
	Northants	1st	b Clarke 24	Livingston c Parr b Lomax 17
		2nd	c Clarke b Brown 1	Davis st Parr b Berry 2
1953	Australians	1st	b Lindwall 4	
	Derbyshire	1st	b Smith 25	Carr c Parr b Tattershall 0
		2nd		Elliott c Parr b Tattershall 19
				Jackson st Parr b Berry 2
	Essex	1st	Did not bat	Cousens st Parr b Berry 3
	Glamorgan	1st	c McConnan b Muneer 15	Pleass c Parr b Tattershall 5

Year	Opponents	Innings	Batting score	Dismissals
	Gloucs	1st	c Hawkins b Mortimore 7	
		2nd		McHugh st Parr b Berry 0
	Kent	1st	c Ridgway b Wright 26	Fagg c Parr b Statham 0
				Ufton c Parr b Smith 39
		2nd		Phebey c Parr b Statham 2
				Mayes c Parr b Smith 16
				Ufton c Parr b Smith 10
				Murray c Parr b Smith 1
				Ridgway c Parr b Statham 0
	Leics	1st	c Spencer b Goodwin 1	Tompkin c Parr b Statham 2
				Palmer st Parr b Berry 48
				Hallam c Parr b Tattershall 3
		2nd		Jackson c Parr b Statham 87
	Middlesex	1st	Did not bat	Robertson c Parr b Statham 13
		2nd		Roberston c Parr b Statham 31
	Northants	1st	Did not bat	Oldfield c Parr b Smith 2
				Tribe c Parr b Smith 3
	Notts	1st	b Dooland 10	Clay c Parr b Statham 108
				Poole c Parr b Statham 1
				Butler c Parr b Statham 7
		2nd		Hardstaff c Parr b Statham 0
	Somerset	1st	Not out 15	Rogers st Parr b Hilton 7
	Sussex	1st	b Wood 7	Langridge c Parr b Hilton 1
				Cox c Parr b Statham 96
		2nd	Run out 29	
	Warwicks	1st	c Horner b Dollery 1	Gardner c Parr b Tattershall 14
	Worcs	1st	Not out 15	Bird st Parr b Berry 34
				Broadbent st Parr b Berry 0
	Yorkshire	1st	c Watson b Wardle 4	Illingworth c Parr b Tattershall 24
		2nd	Not out 21	
	Oxford Univ	1st	Did not bat	Fasken c Parr b Statham 20
	Warwicks	1st	b Dollery 0	Hitchcock c Parr b Wharton 3
		2nd	Run out 2	
	Sussex	1st	c Webb b Cox 7	
		2nd		Cox c Parr b Statham 0
				Oakman c Parr b Tattershall 38
				Thomson st Parr b Hilton 2
	Yorkshire	1st	st Brennan b Halliday 4	Wardle c Parr b Tattershall 1
		2nd	c Yardley b Wardle 0	
	Surrey	1st	b Laker 24	Clark c Parr b Hilton 39
		2nd	c Lock b Bedser 10	
	Derbyshire	1st	Did not bat	

Year	Opponents	Innings	Batting score	Dismissals
	Cambridge Univ	1st	Did not bat	Turner st Parr b Berry 0
	Middlesex	1st	Not out 2	Sharp c Parr b Lomax 26
		2nd		W.Edrich st Parr b G.Edrich 105
	Hampshire	1st	Did not bat	Shackleton c Parr b Statham 3
		2nd		Rogers st Parr b Berry 21
	Glamorgan	1st	C Lewis b Wooller 4	Davies st Parr b Tatteshall 0
		2nd	Not out 4	
	Essex	1st	Did not bat	
	Somerset	1st	Did not bat	
		2nd		Baker c Parr b Smith 10
	Worcs	1st	c Yarnold b Perks 5	Richardson c Parr b Berry 62
		2nd	c Kenyon b Chatterton 5	
	Northants	1st	b Tribe 10	Lightfoot st Parr b Hilton 1
		2nd	c Reynolds b Clarke 10	Broderick c Parr b Statham 8
	Kent	1st	Did not bat	
	For MCC v Yorks	1st	Not out 4	Watson c Parr b Tattershall 38
		2nd	c Cowan b Wardle 10	
1954	Hampshire	1st	c Barnard b Gray 0	
	Warwicks	1st	Not out 16	Dollery c Parr b Statham 1
		2nd		Wolton c Parr b Hilton 26
				Bromley c Parr b Hilton 3
	Pakistan	1st	lbw b Zulfiqar Ahmed 0	Zulfiqar c Parr b Statham 6
		2nd	c Zulfiqar b Shujauddin 13	
	Gloucs	1st	b Cook 4	Rochford st Parr b Greenhough 0
				Wells c Parr b Hilton 8
				Cook st Parr b Hilton 8
		2nd		Milton c Parr b Tattershall 24
	Notts	1st	Did not bat	Clay c Parr b Smith 7

Year	M	Inns	NO	Runs	HS	Av.	Caught	Stumped	Total
1951	2	3	1	11	10*	5.5	2	-	2
1952	12	15	3	182	42	15.16	22	5	27
1953	31	30	6	281	29	11.71	37	13	50
1954	4	3	1	20	16*	10.00	7	2	9
					*not out				
Totals	49	51	11	494	42	12.35	68	20	88

Bibliography

Cardus, Neville, *Cardus on Cricket*, Longmans/Souvenir (1949)

Dankworth, John, *Jazz in Revolution*, Constable (1998)

Frith, David, *The Golden Age of Cricket 1890-1914*, Lutterworth Press (1978)

Gilchrist, Roy, *Hit Me For Six*, Stanley Paul (1963)

Godbolt, Jim, *A History of Jazz in Britain 1919-50*, Quartet (1984)

                 All That and Many a Dog, Quartet/Northway (1986)

                 All This and Slowly Deteriorating Fast, Proper (2013)

Green, Benny, *The Wisden Papers of Neville Cardus*, Stanley Paul (1989)

Green, Jeffrey, *Edmund Jenkins – The Life & Times of an American Black Composer,* Greenwood (1982)

Hughes, Spike, *The Art of Coarse Cricket*, Hutchinson (1961)

                 Opening Bars (1946)

James, C.L.R, *Beyond a Boundary*, Stanley Paul (1963)

Johnston, Brian, *More Views From the Boundary*, Mandarin (1993)

Lewis, Vic, *Music and Maiden Overs*, Chatto & Windus (1987)

Litweiler, John, *The Freedom Principle*, Blandford (1984)

Manley, Michael, *A History of West Indian Cricket*, Andre Deutsch (1995)

Matera, Marc, *Black London – The Imperial Metropolis and Decolonisation in the 20th Century*
    Univ of California Press (2015)

Melly, George, *Owning Up*, Penguin (1965)

Melville, Tom, *The Tented Field – A History of Cricket in America*, Popular Press (1998)

Oliver, Paul (Ed), *Black Music in Britain – Essays on the Afro-Asian Contribution to Popular Music*
    OUP (1990)

Odendaal, Andre, *The Story of an African Game,* David Phillips (2003)

Rayvern Allen, David, *A Song For Cricket*, Pelham Books (1981)

Thompson, Leslie/Green, Jeffrey, *Swing From a Small Island – The Story of Leslie Thompson*, Northway
    (1985)

Toop, David, Into the Maelstrom – *Music, Improvisation and the Dream of Freedom*, Bloomsbury
    (2016)

Turner, Bruce, *Hot Air, Cool Music*, Quartet (1984)

Williams, Jack, *Cricket and Race*, Bloomsbury (2001)

Recommended recordings

Jazz in Britain 1919-1950   Properbox 88

Fred Elizalde   Jazz at the Savoy   Decca ACL1102

Fred Elizalde   Cambridge University Jazz 1927-36   Jazz Oracle BDW8061

Spike Hughes & his All American Orchestra   Decca ACL 1153

Fela Sowande   Africa Heritage Symphonies Series Vol.1   Cedille CDR90000055

Adelaide Hall with Fela Sowande   There Goes That Song Again   Decca RFL3

Black British Swing   Topic TSCD781

Lord Kitchener   Calypso: Sounds of the Caribbean Islands Vol.8   Documents 600311

Vic Lewis Progressive Jazz/Music For Moderns   Vocalion 2004

George Webb's Dixielanders   1943-47   Jazzology J122

Wally Fawkes & The Troglodytes   Flook Digs Jazz   Lake LACD143

Wally Fawkes/Sandy Brown/Bruce Turner   Juicy & Full Toned   Lake LACD12

George Melly /Mick Mulligan Band   Doom   Cherry Red ACMEM273CD

Bruce Turner   Jump Band Collection   Lake LACD184

Bruce Turner/John Barnes   Jazz Masters   Cadillac SGC1005

Campbell Burnap   Night Working   Mainstem MCD0010

George Shearing   Lullaby of Birdland (1947-52)   Naxos 8120823

John Dankworth   Bop in Britain Vol.1   Jasmine JASCD 637

John Dankworth   Spread a Little Happiness   Avid AMSC854

Tony Crombie/Tubby Hayes   Jazz at the Flamingo   Jasmine JASCD 618

Johnny Barnes/Roy Williams   The Outswingers   Swing Out

Orlando Le Fleming   From Brooklyn With Love   19/8Records

Orlando Le Fleming   Romantic Funk: The Unfamiliar   Whirlwind WR4763

Just Not Jazz – 3 Days of British Improvised Music in Berlin   NVNC-LP001/004

Chris Corsano   The Young Cricketer   CD (no details)

Index